Euripides

Iphigeneia at Aulis

A new translation and
commentary by Holly Eckhardt
and John Harrison

Introduction to the Greek Theatre
by P. E. Easterling

Series Editors: John Harrison and Judith Affleck

D1053554

CAMBRIDGE
UNIVERSITY PRESS

CAMBRIDGE UNIVERSITY PRESS
Cambridge, New York, Melbourne, Madrid, Cape Town,
Singapore, São Paulo, Delhi, Mexico City

Cambridge University Press
The Edinburgh Building, Cambridge CB2 8RU, UK

www.cambridge.org
Information on this title: www.cambridge.org/9781107601161

First published 2012

Printed in India by Replika Press Pvt. Ltd

A catalogue record for this publication is available from the British Library

ISBN 978-1-107-60116-1 Paperback

ACKNOWLEDGEMENTS
The authors and publishers acknowledge the following sources of copyright material
and are grateful for the permissions granted.

Cover – Perrier, François dit le Bourguignon, *Le Sacrifice d'Iphigénie*, inv 4931
© Musée des Beaux-Arts de Dijon, photo Hugo Mertens

p. viii AF Archive/Alamy; p. 9 bpk/Antikensammlung, Staatliche Museen zu
Berlin/Johannes Laurentius; p. 11 ClassicStock/Alamy; pp. 14, 31, 44, 62, 80 Geraint
Lewis; pp. 48, 86, 90, 105 Greek Film Centre/Kobal Collection; p. 98 Robert Harding
Picture Library/SuperStock

Contents

Preface

The aim of the series is to enable students to approach Classical plays with confidence and understanding: to discover the play within the text.

The translations are new. Many recent versions of Greek tragedy have been produced by poets and playwrights who do not work from the original Greek. The translators of this series aim to bring readers, actors and directors as close as possible to the playwrights' actual words and intentions: to create translations which are faithful to the original in content and tone; and which are speakable, with all the immediacy of modern English.

The notes are designed for students of Classical Civilisation and Drama, and indeed anyone who is interested in theatre. They address points which present difficulty to the reader of today: chiefly relating to the Greeks' religious and moral attitudes, their social and political life, and mythology.

Our hope is that students should discover the play for themselves. The conventions of the Classical theatre are discussed, but there is no thought of recommending 'authentic' performances. Different groups will find different ways of responding to each play. The best way of bringing alive an ancient play, as any other, is to explore the text practically, to stimulate thought about ways of staging the plays today. Stage directions in the text are minimal, and the notes are not prescriptive; rather, they contain questions and exercises which explore the dramatic qualities of the text. Bullet points introduce suggestions for discussion and analysis; open bullet points focus on more practical exercises.

If the series encourages students to attempt a staged production, so much the better. But the primary aim is understanding and enjoyment.

This translation of *Iphigeneia at Aulis* is based on the Greek text edited by J. Diggle for Oxford University Press.

John Harrison
Judith Affleck

Background to the story of Iphigeneia at Aulis

THE JUDGEMENT OF PARIS

Zeus had fallen in love with the sea-nymph Thetis when he received a prophecy from Prometheus the Titan that the son of Thetis was destined to be more powerful than his father. Fearing that his position as king of the gods was threatened, Zeus arranged for Thetis to be married to a mortal, so that her son would also be mortal. So Thetis was betrothed to the mortal Peleus.

The wedding of Peleus and Thetis was a joyous occasion to which all the gods and goddesses were invited, with one exception. Eris, the goddess of quarrel, had been excluded for fear that she would spoil the happy event. When she found out about the wedding, she turned up unexpectedly at the feast to bring her present for the happy couple. Her gift was a golden apple bearing the inscription 'For the fairest'. The goddesses Hera, queen of the gods, Athena, goddess of wisdom, and Aphrodite, goddess of love, all claimed that the golden apple was rightfully theirs and it was decided that an impartial judge should be sought. Paris, the most handsome mortal, a Trojan prince who was then a shepherd on Mount Ida near Troy, was chosen for the job. Each goddess offered Paris a reward if he were to pick her. Hera offered him power, Athena offered him wisdom, and Aphrodite offered him the most beautiful woman in the world. Paris awarded the golden apple to Aphrodite, and as a result he was promised Helen, who was not only the most beautiful woman, but also the wife of King Menelaus of Sparta.

Paris set off to claim his reward. When he arrived in Sparta, Menelaus was away from home in Crete, and Paris took Helen home with him to Troy – either willingly or by force. When Menelaus returned, he and his brother Agamemnon raised an expedition against Troy to recover Helen. So the judgement of Paris can be said to have been the cause of the Trojan War.

THE UPBRINGING OF ACHILLES

The son born to Peleus and Thetis was Achilles. When he was a baby, according to some versions, his mother tried to make him immortal by dipping him in the river Styx, but he was still vulnerable in the heel, by which she held him. Peleus sent his son to be educated by his old tutor, the Centaur Cheiron, on Mount Pelion. As the Greek armies were gathering for the expedition to Troy, Thetis, knowing that Achilles might either live a long and inglorious life or win glory at Troy and die young, disguised him as a girl and hid him at the court of King Lycomedes on the island of Scyros, to try to save him from going to war. During his time on Scyros, the princess Deidameia bore him a son,

Neoptolemus. Because the Greeks needed Achilles' prowess, Odysseus tracked him down on Scyros, where he left some armour in the women's quarters. Achilles betrayed himself by the interest with which he handled it, and joined the fleet as it gathered at Aulis.

The first production of Iphigeneia at Aulis

Euripides left Athens in 408 BC to go to live at the court of King Achelaus of Macedonia, where he died two years later. His old rival Sophocles led the mourning for him at the festival of Dionysia in Athens. Three of his plays received their first performance posthumously: *Iphigeneia at Aulis*, *Alcmaeon in Corinth* (now lost) and *Bacchae*, probably in 405 BC. They were awarded the first prize, for only the fifth time in a long career. There is some evidence that they were produced by Euripides' son; it is not certain whether the plays were finished when the dramatist died.

A note on the text

Iphigeneia has survived thanks to a single printed manuscript (Venice, 1503). There are more uncertainties about this text than most of Euripides' plays and it is possible that changes – including additions – were made even before the first performance. The unusual structure of the Prologue suggests to some that there may have originally been two versions. The ending too – from the Messenger's entry – has also been questioned, especially the passage relating the 'miracle' (1537–end). The text as it stands certainly has unusual features, but none seems impossible for such an innovative dramatist as Euripides; in its present state it makes for powerful stage performance.

Further reading

The authors would like to acknowledge help in particular from Pantelis Michelakis, *Iphigeneia at Aulis*, London, Bloomsbury, 2006.

D.J. Conacher, *Euripidean Drama: Myth, Theme and Structure*, London, Oxford University Press, 1967.

S. Goldhill, *Reading Greek Tragedy*, Cambridge, Cambridge University Press, 1986.

J. Morwood, *The Plays of Euripides*, London, Bloomsbury, 2004.

O. Taplin, *Greek Tragedy in Action*, London, Methuen, 1978.

Map of Ancient Greece

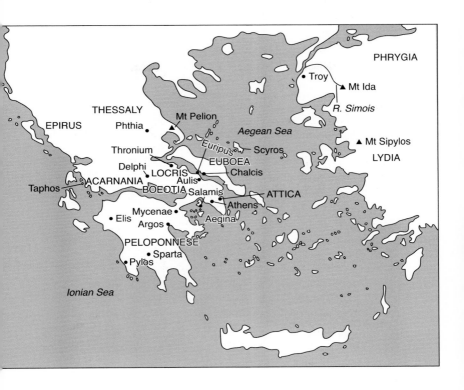

Clytaemnestra and Iphigeneia (from Cacoyannis' film Ifigeneia, *1977)*

List of characters

AGAMEMNON · *king of Argos and commander of the expedition against Troy*

OLD MAN · *a slave, servant of Agamemnon*

CHORUS · *young married women of Chalcis*

MENELAUS · *king of Sparta, brother of Agamemnon and husband of Helen*

MESSENGER 1 · *from Argos, in Clytaemnestra's entourage*

CLYTAEMNESTRA · *wife of Agamemnon*

IPHIGENEIA · *daughter of Agamemnon and Clytaemnestra*

ACHILLES · *prince of Phthia, leader of the Myrmidons*

MESSENGER 2 · *a soldier sent by Agamemnon*

PROLOGUE (1–157)

The Prologue is the part of a Greek play that precedes the entry of the Chorus. Euripides rarely begins a play as he does here, with a dramatic dialogue between two characters. He usually starts with a single character who gives the background to the situation, in the way Agamemnon does in lines 49–114. The two sections of dialogue, lines 1–48 and 115–57, which frame Agamemnon's speech are in an anapaestic rhythm, used for animated speech. Agamemnon's long speech is in iambic trimeters, the usual metre of tragic dialogue.

Setting of the play

The action takes place in a single day in Aulis, on the Boeotian side of the Euripus strait which separates the island of Euboea from the Greek mainland (see map, p. vii). The Greek fleet had assembled here ready to set sail to wage war against Troy. The army is unable to sail because of the lack of wind (10), and so the Greeks have set up a temporary camp of makeshift tents (1) while they wait for more favourable conditions.

Agamemnon the leader

Agamemnon, son of Atreus (29), is a major character in the story of the Trojan War. As leader of the Greek campaign, he plays a prominent role in the *Iliad* and in Greek tragedy. In the *Iliad* he is presented as a brave fighter but a flawed character: aggressive, quarrelsome and also irresolute. However, Euripides always felt free to adapt characters to his own design. Here Agamemnon is shown in private, with his slave, in a state of agitation.

6 What is that bright star This star is probably Sirius (which is the Greek word for 'bright'), the Dog Star, visible in the hottest days of summer. The Pleiades are a constellation of seven stars. The stars were important to the Greeks for navigation and play a large role in myths. This reference both fixes the action in summer time (though the play was performed in the spring) and adds a note of foreboding. Sirius was for Homer a sign of evil, bringing fever.

Burden of responsibility (17–23)

In Greek literature there is often a tension between an individual's public responsibilities to the community and private obligations to their family. As a leader Agamemnon has a duty to his men, but this is accompanied by its own pressures (23).

AGAMEMNON Old Man, come out of the tent.

OLD MAN I'm coming. What are you up to now, Lord Agamemnon?

AGAMEMNON Hurry!

OLD MAN I'm coming, I'm coming.
There's no rest for the aged; my eyes are sore.

AGAMEMNON What is that bright star I see
Still shining in mid-heaven,
Crossing the Pleiades with their seven paths?
There's no sound either of birds
Or of the sea. The silence of the wind
Grips the strait.

OLD MAN Why are you rushing about out here,
Agamemnon?
All is still quiet over Aulis
And the guards on the walls have not moved.
Let's go inside.

AGAMEMNON I envy you, Old Man, and I envy any man
Who lives life free from danger, unnoticed and obscure.
Those in authority I envy less.

OLD MAN But status makes for a good life.

AGAMEMNON Yes, but that good life is slippery:
Honour may be sweet,
But it brings suffering.

Demands of religion

The Greeks did not have a word for 'religion'; the notion of 'piety' (*eusebeia*) comes closest to the idea – the need to appease the powerful but volatile gods, who were thought to resent human success and prosperity. Mortals must avoid exceeding their proper human limits in their dealings with gods or men (*hubris*). Piety was concerned with the performance of traditional rituals and the observance of traditional modes of restrained behaviour and thought. 'Neglect of the gods' (24) risked punishment (*nemesis*) or retribution from the gods. In Euripides' *Bacchae*, Pentheus, king of Thebes, refuses to worship the god Dionysus. The god asserts his power, driving the women of Thebes into a frenzy in which Pentheus is torn to pieces by his own mother. Caution requires that mortals should always try to ascertain the gods' will (90).

Nobility

The Greeks expected those of noble birth (line 28) to display all-round excellence (*aretē*), including superior moral qualities, and thus fulfil their obligations to the wider community. In the heroic code of the *Iliad*, heroes fought for glory and honour, accepting their lot without complaint. Tragic heroines too responded to the demands of nobility: Antigone in Sophocles' *Antigone* chooses to die rather than renounce her religious and family obligations; and Polyxena in Euripides' *Hecuba* chooses death rather than the life of a slave. Agamemnon's questioning of his role (17–19, 21–3) marks him out from the conventional hero. See **'Honour and reputation'**, p. 28.

30 You are mortal Achilles, speaking to Priam at the end of the *Iliad*, declares that no mortal can live without some misfortune. See **'The human condition'**, p. 14 (also 156).

35 this tablet in your hand The writing tablet was probably a wooden booklet, hinged down the middle, and could be sealed on the outside. The inside probably contained smooth wax on which a message could be etched. It is an important prop in the play, and will feature again (110, 284–305).

45 an honest and trustworthy man In Euripides' plays the humble characters, such as the Old Man here, a long-standing slave of the family (46–8), are often depicted as wise and loyal.

Sometimes neglect of the gods
Topples a man's life,   25
Sometimes the ruthless criticism of our fellow men
Crushes it to pieces.

OLD MAN I don't like to hear a man of noble birth talk like this.
Agamemnon, Atreus did not father you for blessings from start
    to finish.
You are mortal,   30
Born for pain as well as joy,
Whether you like it or not.
That is the will of the gods.
But here you are,
With this tablet in your hand, writing away   35
By torch light,
Rubbing out and rewriting what you've already written,
Opening and resealing it
And weeping heavy tears;
And then you throw it to the ground.   40
You seem to have taken leave of your senses.
What's tormenting you?
What is this new problem?
Come now, share it with me.
You'll be speaking to an honest and trustworthy man.   45

46 Tyndareus The father of Clytaemnestra, Agamemnon's wife (47).
See **'Leda's children'** below.

Marriage and dowries

When a young Greek girl married, she passed from the authority of her
father to that of her husband. The legal contract was sealed with a dowry
(47), usually a chest containing a sum of money or valuables which was
held in trust for her throughout her married life. The bride's family
would provide this. Here the dowry included the gift of an old servant.

Agamemnon's speech

The naturalistic dialogue is interrupted by a long speech giving
background information necessary for the audience, but probably
largely familiar to the Old Man. This structure is unusual, but in
performance seems to present no difficulty (see *A note on the text*, p. vi).

Leda's children

Tyndareus and his wife Leda had four children: the twin boys Castor
and Pollux (see 742n) and Clytaemnestra and Helen. In most accounts
Zeus was the father of the twins and of Helen; in the form of a swan he
seduced Leda, and Helen hatched from an egg laid by her mother.
Phoebe (50) is not often mentioned as one of Leda's daughters.

Tyndareus' predicament

An unmarried girl was considered to be under the power of her father,
and it would have been for Tyndareus to decide which suitor would
marry his daughter. As the competition to woo Helen was fierce, the
suitors' emotions were running dangerously high (53–4) and Tyndareus
had to find a way to resolve the situation amicably.

Oaths, sacrifices and libations

Oaths in the ancient world were not taken lightly; an oath was a sworn
vow made in the name of the gods, and Zeus was the deity responsible
for them. In a largely oral society, agreements were made under oath
and the gods acted as guarantors to such agreements. Such contracts
were then sealed, as commonly now, by the shaking of hands (59).
Sacrifices (60), of the first fruits of a harvest or a young animal, and
libations (61), the pouring out of milk, wine or olive oil on to the
ground, were performed to encourage the gods to witness the
agreement.

65 Greek or barbarian See **'Barbarians and Troy'**, p. 8.

For long ago, Tyndareus
Sent me to your wife as part of her dowry,
An honest attendant for the bride.

AGAMEMNON Leda, daughter of Thestius, had three daughters,
Phoebe, Clytaemnestra, my wife,   50
And Helen. The most prosperous young men of Greece
Came as suitors to Helen.
There arose great jealousy among them and
Each uttered dreadful threats against the others,
Should he not get the girl.   55
It was hard for her father Tyndareus to know
Whether to give her or not to give her, how best to handle the situation.
And this solution came to him:
That the suitors should take oaths, clasp hands
And, with burnt sacrifices,   60
Pour out libations and swear that,
No matter who won Tyndareus' daughter as his wife,
They should all unite to help him, if any man should take her
    from her home.
And they should wage war against that man
And destroy his city, be it Greek or barbarian,   65
If he should drive her husband from the marriage bed.

70 the sweet breath of Aphrodite In early Greek thought, passion was linked to a deity. The name of Aphrodite, the Greek goddess of love, is a metonym here, standing for sexual desire. Tyndareus allows Helen to choose her own husband (69) according to her fancy, and so relieves himself of the responsibility of making a decision.

71 Menelaus Brother of Agamemnon and king of Sparta.

72 Paris . . . beauty contest See *Background to the story*, p. v.

Barbarians and Troy

Homer does not talk of 'barbarians' in the *Iliad*; the Trojans were as civilised as the Greeks. But after their success in repelling the Persian invasions, the Greeks tended to look down on those who came from the east. 'Barbarian' (originally one who could not speak Greek, but seemed to say 'ba-ba-ba') is a fifth-century BC word. Agamemnon adopts the attitudes of many of Euripides' contemporaries, who would have viewed themselves as free and civilised, and classed Asians as slaves, luxurious ('barbarian splendour', 74), emotional, cruel and immoral (see 1365–6).

75 He lusted after Helen, and she for him Agamemnon states that Helen was not an unwilling victim of abduction, but that she and Paris had mutual feelings, and so she bears some responsibility for the consequences. See **'Helen's guilt'**, p. 54.

Guest-friendship

The early Greeks set up networks of guest-friends as they travelled the ancient world. They formed bonds of trust (*xenia*) that required them to offer hospitality and help to their guests and hosts. *Xenia* was protected by Zeus, and anyone who broke the rules of hospitality would be punished for their *hubris* (see **'Demands of religion'**, p. 4). Paris broke the rules by seducing Helen, his host Menelaus' wife (76). (See *Background to the story*, p. v.) The Greeks are now seeking their revenge.

77 his cow-shed on Ida Ida is the mountain range close to Troy. Agamemnon's choice of words reflects his contempt for Paris.

81 the Greeks sprang up, armed and ready for battle The language here is reminiscent of Homer, and recalls the arming scenes of the *Iliad*.

85 they chose me to lead Agamemnon's sentiments towards leadership here (87) recall his earlier words (17–23).

And when they had pledged themselves – how well old
Tyndareus got round them with his shrewd mind –
He allowed his daughter to choose from the suitors the one
To whom the sweet breath of Aphrodite drew her.   70
And she chose Menelaus. If only he'd rejected her!
The story goes that Paris, who had been the judge
Of the goddesses' beauty contest, came to Sparta from Troy,
Flamboyant in his style of dress and gleaming with gold,
      barbarian splendour.
He lusted after Helen, and she for him,   75
And when Menelaus was away from home, he seduced her
And returned to his cow-shed on Ida.
Menelaus, enraged, rushed round Greece,
And he reminded people of their former oaths to Tyndareus,
Saying that they must help those who have been wronged.   80
At this the Greeks sprang up, armed and ready for battle,
And came to the base here at Aulis with its narrow strait,
With many ships and armour,
And squadrons of horse and chariots.
And they chose me to lead the campaign   85
Out of respect for Menelaus, since I was his brother.
I wish that someone else had received this honour instead of me!
When the army had mustered and assembled,
We sat idle around Aulis, unable to sail.

Hermes leads the three goddesses Aphrodite, Athene and Hera to Paris
for his judgement (Attic vase, Berlin).

Calchas' prophecy

The Greek army, assembled at Aulis, is unable to sail because there is no wind (10, 332). As the Greeks believed that natural phenomena were controlled by the gods, Calchas (90), their principal seer, was asked to interpret the lack of wind. He pronounced the need for a sacrifice to Artemis. The reason given for this varies. In Aeschylus' *Agamemnon*, Artemis, protector of life, demands that, before the fleet can sail, the Greek commander should make a sacrifice in advance for all the suffering the Greeks will cause in Troy. Elsewhere (e.g. Sophocles' *Electra*) Agamemnon must make amends for killing a stag sacred to Artemis and boasting of it. Here Euripides is not interested in the reason for Artemis' demand. Calchas simply states (93) that a sacrifice will make the expedition possible; there is no suggestion (94) that failure to sacrifice will anger Artemis. The Greeks have a choice and it can be decided on human terms, by the conflicting claims of family and duty. The Greek text does not make clear to whom Calchas announced the prophecy (see **'Secrecy and lies'**, p. 12, 493n, 504).

Agamemnon's children

Agamemnon was the father of Clytaemnestra's four children: Iphigeneia, Chrysothemis, Electra and Orestes. Only Iphigeneia and the baby Orestes appear in this play.

92 Artemis Goddess of wildlife, hunting and child-birth. Her virgin status means that she also protects the innocent, such as the unborn child. Artemis had a sanctuary at Brauron, 17 km from Athens, and there was also a temple to Artemis at Aulis, a popular tourist attraction. The fact that she demands a human sacrifice to allow the fleet to sail is unusual, but it is a traditional feature of the story; goats or deer were the usual sacrificial animals for Artemis.

Human sacrifice

Although there is archaeological evidence that the Minoan and Mycenaean Greeks (1800–1100 BC) performed human sacrifices in times of great peril, the Greeks of the fifth century BC encountered stories of human sacrifice only in tragedy.

95 Talthybius Agamemnon's herald. It was the job of a herald to issue formal proclamations, keep order at meetings and carry messages.

101 Achilles Achilles, king of Phthia in Thessaly (see map, p. vii), joined the expedition with 50 ships and his contingent of Myrmidons (222, *Iliad* 2). For his upbringing see *Background to the story*, p. v.

In our perplexity, Calchas the prophet announced the gods' will: 90
That I must sacrifice my own child, Iphigeneia,
To Artemis who has her sanctuary here,
And that, if we sacrifice, Troy will be destroyed;
But without the sacrifice this will not be.
When I heard this, I ordered Talthybius 95
With a loud proclamation to dismiss the whole army,
As I could never bring myself to kill my own daughter.
At this my brother, employing every kind of argument,
Prevailed on me to do something terrible.
I sent a letter to my wife, 100
Telling her to send our daughter, to be married to Achilles.

The goddess Artemis.

Wedding feasts

As part of the Greek wedding ritual, there was normally a wedding feast at the house of the bride's father. Both families would have been present. As Agamemnon and the bridegroom Achilles are both stationed at Aulis, the bride has been summoned. See **'Greek marriage customs'**, p. 32.

107 Odysseus King of Ithaca, renowned for his cunning, trickery and invention (see **'Odysseus'**, p. 38).

Change of mind

Initially Agamemnon did not even consider the idea of killing his daughter (97), but in the space of two lines he changed his mind (99). He has now changed his mind again and written a second letter (109–11).

Secrecy and lies

In order to get Iphigeneia to Aulis, Agamemnon ties himself in a web of deceit. He orders Talthybius to dismiss the army, but does not publicise the prophecy, which is known only to a close group of three confidants (107, 493n, 504). Then – persuaded by his brother (98–9) – he sends a letter telling his wife to send Iphigeneia to a (sham) wedding. The way in which he refers to the letter (101) suggests that he did not invite Clytaemnestra (105, 436). He then writes a second letter, cancelling the first (117), but keeps this secret from his confidants (110–12).

111 Argos City in the north-east Peloponnese (see map, p. vii) and kingdom of Agamemnon.

Achilles' anger

The Old Man is quick to point out Agamemnon's lack of respect for Achilles, involving his name in the deceit (123–34). Achilles' fiery temper is a conspicuous feature of the *Iliad* and, as Agamemnon begins to realise (135–6), he will regret this thoughtless mistake.

130 To cradle The metaphor makes Iphigeneia seem very young and vulnerable.

I boasted about the man's worthiness
And said that he would not sail with the Greeks
Unless a bride from our family went to Phthia.
That's the argument I used to persuade my wife,   105
Inventing a sham marriage for my daughter.
Calchas, Odysseus and Menelaus are the only Greeks
Apart from me who know this. But I was wrong
To do it. I've changed my mind and written
This second letter – the one you saw me sealing and resealing   110
In the night. Take it and go to Argos.
What I've written is a secret, but I'll tell you
What it says, because you are
Loyal to my wife and family.

OLD MAN Yes, tell me, then what I say   115
Will match the letter.

AGAMEMNON I am sending this letter to cancel
The last. 'Daughter of Leda,
Do NOT send your daughter to Euboea,
To the sheltered bay of Aulis.   120
We'll have our daughter's wedding feast another time.'

OLD MAN But surely, if he's robbed of his marriage,
Achilles will rage and be indignant
With you and your wife.
This is dangerous. What are you saying?   125

AGAMEMNON Achilles plays no part in this beyond his name.
He knows nothing of the marriage, nor
What we are up to, nor that I have promised
To give my child to him
To cradle in his marriage bed.   130

OLD MAN That was a dangerous game, my lord –
To promise your daughter to the son of a goddess,
When you were bringing her here to be
A sacrifice for the Greeks.

AGAMEMNON Yes! I was out of my mind.   135
I could be ruined. On your way. Get moving.
Forget you're old!

153 Helios' chariot Helios was the god of the sun, and is often depicted in Greek art driving his chariot across the sky to represent time passing.

The human condition

It was a commonplace of Greek thought that status, success and wealth do not guarantee happiness (see 20–7). The proverb 'Call no man happy till he is dead' was illustrated by the downfall of rich men such as Croesus and rulers such as Oedipus (*Oedipus Tyrannus*) and Creon (*Antigone*). Agamemnon's words (156–7) about the happiness and grief that humans encounter are reminiscent of the Old Man's earlier advice to him (31–2).

The Prologue

- What impression do you get of Agamemnon's character?
- What impression do you get of the Old Man and his relationship with his master?

PARODOS (ENTRY OF THE CHORUS) (158–279)

The Chorus were highly trained male singers and dancers who often wore lavish costumes. At the time of *Iphigeneia at Aulis*, there were 15 members in a tragic chorus. They entered from the sides (*parodoi*) and performed in the *orchēstra* (see p. 113); they were present throughout the action. They sang in unison, but when the Chorus were involved in dialogue with other characters the Chorus leader spoke. The chorus in Euripides' plays is usually linked to one of the characters. However this Chorus is made up of young, married women from the town of Chalcis across the water from the Greek camp at Aulis, where there is a contingent from Chalcis (*Iliad* 2). They have heard from their husbands (167, 276) about the army and its famous heroes who, unable to set sail, pass the time in sport and recreation. An army camp was no place for women, so there is a sense of bravado in their going as sight-seers to spy on the men.

161 Arethusa A fountain of Chalcis.

166 demi-gods This Greek word occurs in the *Iliad* and shows that many of the Greek heroes had divine parentage.

The Chorus (National Theatre, London, 2004; director Katie Mitchell).

OLD MAN I will hurry, majesty.

AGAMEMNON No resting by the spring in the wood,
   No falling asleep!   140

OLD MAN Of course not!

AGAMEMNON When you come to a fork on the way,
   Make sure you don't miss a carriage
   Speeding past, carrying my daughter here
   To the Greek fleet.   145

OLD MAN I will.

AGAMEMNON If you meet her escort leaving the gates
   Of Argos, rein them round
   Straight back into the city.

OLD MAN But when I give my message how shall I   150
   Make myself believed by your daughter and your wife?

AGAMEMNON Keep the seal unbroken on the letter. Off you go!
   Dawn and the fire of Helios' chariot
   Begin to show, bringing up the light.
   Help me through this difficulty!   155
   No one prospers or is happy to the end of life.
   No man has yet been born without his share of grief.

CHORUS   I have come along the sandy beach
       Of Aulis, along the water's edge.
         I left my city, Chalcis,   160
  Which nurses famous Arethusa's water close by the sea,
         And came across the waves
         Of the strait of Euripus,
        To see the army of the Greeks
     And the banks of oars that drive the ships   165
        Of the Greek demi-gods.
        Our husbands tell us that
    Fair Menelaus and the noble Agamemnon
      Will launch a thousand ships
         Against Troy   170
        In search of Helen.

173 Eurotas The river on whose banks Sparta was built.

175 the goddess of Cyprus Aphrodite was thought to have been born from the sea at Paphos in Cyprus.

177 the beauty contest Between Aphrodite, Hera and Pallas Athene (178, 234n). See *Background to the story*, p. v.

179 the grove of Artemis For Artemis and her cult see 92n. The Chorus are keen to observe what is going on (183), but they are also aware of the code of proper, modest behaviour (181) for women.

186 the two Ajaxes There were two heroes among the Greek warriors called Ajax. Ajax, son of Oileus, chief of the Locrians, was often known as 'lesser'. Ajax, son of Telamon, was famous for his great size and bulk. After the death of Achilles much later in the war, while Ajax was rescuing his body, Odysseus held back the Trojans. His reward was Achilles' armour. Ajax went mad with anger, killed the Greeks' herds, and then committed suicide (see Sophocles' *Ajax*).

188 Salamis An island separated by a narrow strait from the south-west coast of Attica, near Athens' harbour at Piraeus (see map, p. vii). In September 480 BC the Greeks defeated Persia here in a naval battle. It was also the birthplace of Euripides.

189 Protesilaus sitting with Palamedes Protesilaus was the leader of a contingent from Thessaly. When they reached Troy, he was the first to disembark, and was killed.

191 a game of draughts According to the Greek travel writer Pausanias, Palamedes invented the games of draughts and dice to while away the hours of the Trojan War.

192 Diomedes Leader of the contingent from Argos and Tiryns and famous warrior of the *Iliad*.

194 Meriones A Greek hero who, according to some traditions, was a suitor of Helen, and so bound by oath to fight (see 59).

196 Laertes' son Odysseus (107n); Euripides uses his patronymic. His homeland, Ithaca, is often presented as a craggy island.

198 Nireus Famous for his beauty, proverbial in Lucian's *Dialogues*.

The herdsman Paris took her,
From the reedy banks of Eurotas,
A gift from Aphrodite,
When the goddess of Cyprus,   175
By the dewy waters,
Won the beauty contest – that contest! –
With Hera and Pallas.

Through the grove of Artemis,
Where many sacrifices have been made,   180
My cheek pink with youthful blushes
I have come, excited,
In my eagerness to see
The armoury of their shields, the warriors' camp
And the throng of horses.   185
I have seen the two Ajaxes sitting together,
One, the son of Oileus,
The other, Telamon's son, the crown of Salamis.
And Protesilaus sitting with Palamedes, grandson of Poseidon,
Delighting in the intricate moves   190
Of a game of draughts.
I saw Diomedes,
Enjoying the sport of discus-throwing,
And next to him Meriones,
Son of Ares, a wonder for mortal eyes.   195
I saw Laertes' son,
Who has come from his island crags,
And with him Nireus,
The most handsome of the Greeks.

Achilles the swift-footed

This first picture that we have of Achilles (200–18), given by the women of Chalcis, is characteristic of the epic hero: a consummate athlete, able, fully armed, to keep pace with a four-horse chariot. Homer often uses the epithet 'swift-footed' to describe him in the *Iliad*.

Chariot-racing

This was a popular – and dangerous – sport at the Greek games. Chariots were decorated and painted, inlaid with ivory and fitted with bronze or even silver, and the wheels were made of elm or willow. In battle a chariot was usually drawn by two horses, one on either side of the pole, by means of a yoke. In races there were usually four horses. The additional horses were attached to either side of the yoked horses by traces. The race was up and down a hair-pin track with a very narrow turn (215); a race was usually 12 laps long. Here a chariot is being put to use in a recreational, but nevertheless competitive, way.

Catalogue of ships 1

The women want also to see the fleet of a thousand ships (169), of which their husbands have talked (167). Now they provide a list of details about these ships. Such lists, or catalogues, recur in Greek literature, as in *Iliad* 2 where the ships of the Greek fleet are listed, and in *Iliad* 3 where Helen provides for Priam, the aged Trojan king, details about the Greek heroes who are fighting around his city's walls.

222 Myrmidons See 673n.

226 Nereids, goddesses The sea-nymphs, including Thetis, were the daughters of the god Nereus. It is appropriate that Achilles chooses them to be his ships' figure-heads.

230 Mekisteus' son Euryalus, one of Diomedes' (192) contingent.

231 Sthenelus the son of Capaneus Sthenelus fought alongside Diomedes (192) and was one of the Greeks who hid in the wooden horse at the capture of Troy. Capaneus was famous for his vast size and strength.

233 son of Theseus Theseus was the legendary founder of Athens. His son's name Acamas and his 60 ships are recorded in Homer's catalogue.

234 the goddess Pallas Pallas Athene was the patron goddess of Athens, which was in Attica (234). The theatre of Dionysus (see *Introduction to the Greek Theatre*, pp. 112–15) was situated at the foot of the Acropolis in the shadow of her temple, the Parthenon. It is fitting that Athene gets a special mention at a performance in her city.

235 winged chariot Athene has another epithet, *Nikē* or Victory. Here, on Acamas' ships, Athene is depicted in a winged chariot, suggesting the speed of victory.

And Achilles I saw, so fast, swift as the wind, 200
    Born to Thetis, trained by Cheiron,
    Running along the sea-shore
    Fully armed.
    He was racing on foot
    Against a four-horse chariot, 205
    Whirling along to out-run it.
    And the driver Eumelus,
    The son of Pheretias,
    Roared on his horses,
Handsome colts, their bridles decked with gold, 210
    And spurred them on with his whip –
The yoke horses dappled, with grizzled manes,
    The trace horses red-maned
    And piebald to their fetlocks –
When they came to the turn in the course. 215
    Beside them bounded Achilles
    Level with the chariot rail,
    Next to the hub of the wheel.

    I tried to count the ships,
    A sight beyond description, 220
    To fill our women's eyes with joy.
The fleet of the Myrmidons from Phthia
    Held the right wing
    With fifty swift ships.
    On the stern, right at the end, 225
Stood golden figurines of Nereids, goddesses,
    The emblem of Achilles' fleet.
With equal numbers were stationed next
    The Argive ships, their admirals
Mekisteus' son, reared by his father Talaus, 230
    And Sthenelus the son of Capaneus.
    Next in line was moored
    The son of Theseus with sixty ships
From Attica, with the goddess Pallas
    Set on a winged chariot, horse-drawn, 235
    An auspicious sight for the sailors.

239 Cadmus The legendary founder of Thebes, a city in Boeotia, is often associated with snakes or dragons. He founded the city of Thebes by sowing the teeth of a dragon he had slain; men sprang from the sown teeth. In Euripides' *Bacchae*, Cadmus is given a prophecy by Dionysus whereby both he and his wife would be turned into snakes for a period of time before going to the underworld, because they failed to acknowledge the god and his worship.

242 Oileus' son See 186n.

244 From Mycenae, built by Cyclopes The city of Agamemnon, Atreus' son, whose walls were made of huge boulders. The Greeks believed that only the Cyclopes had the strength to move such boulders into position. In Euripides' time Mycenae was part of the territory of Argos and the dramatists use both names.

246 His fellow leader was his brother Menelaus (71n).

250 Pylos Kingdom of Nestor (see 251n) in the south-west corner of the Peloponnese (see map, p. vii).

251 Nestor of Gerana The wise, aged king of Pylos. In the *Iliad* he is said to have outlived two generations, yet his mental and physical strength remained intact. He gives much advice, most of it anecdotal, to the Greeks.

252 Alpheus One of the largest rivers in Greece, rising in Arcadia in the centre of the Peloponnese and flowing to the Ionian Sea.

255 Gouneus King of Kyphos, Dodona in Epirus. In *Iliad* 2 he is said to have contributed 22 ships to the expedition.

256 Elis A Greek state in the north-west Peloponnese.

258 Eurytus One of a pair of twins (his brother was Cteatus) who aided King Augeias of Elis (see 256n) when Herakles threatened to invade the state. In return for their help, the king promised them a share in the kingdom.

I saw the Boeotian ships of war,
        Fifty dressed with flags.
    These had on their sterns Cadmus,
        A golden serpent in his hand.   240
    The earth-born Leitus was their commander;
    And Oileus' son led as many Locrian ships,
        Sailing from the famous city Thronium.

From Mycenae, built by Cyclopes, the son of Atreus
    Sent a contingent of one hundred ships.   245
        His fellow leader was his brother,
        Kinsmen together, so that Greece
        Could exact revenge on his wife
    Who fled his home for a foreign marriage.
        From Pylos I saw the ships   250
            Of Nestor of Gerana,
        Their figurehead the river Alpheus
            With the feet of a bull.

    The Aenianians had twelve ships
        Led by their king Gouneus.   255
    And next to them were the lords of Elis,
        Whom everyone called Epeians,
            Led by Eurytus.

260 Taphians The Homeric island of Taphos lay in the Ionian Sea off the coast of Acarnania in north-west Greece (see map, p. vii).

260 Meges King of Dulichium, an island created by Homer, and whose exact location is not known. His father was Phyleus, eldest son of King Augeias, who left his homeland after a dispute with his father and settled in Dulichium.

264 Ajax, reared at Salamis Ajax, son of Telamon (see 186n).

Catalogue of ships 2
The Chorus' catalogue includes 384 ships in the groups that are enumerated. In all the total is probably short of the thousand first envisaged (169). Their extensive knowledge about the ships comes in part from what they have heard at home (275–7).

The *Parodos*
This entry song is much longer than was usual for Euripides. The Chorus express admiration and awe for the glamour and power of the Greek army and fleet. They create a sense of the magnitude of the enterprise on which the Greeks are embarking, an epic background against which we shall view the actions of the leaders and the army.
- What is the attitude of the Chorus to what they have seen?
- What do we gain from having the viewpoint of young, married women?
- What do we learn about the women themselves from their description of the scene?
- How appropriate do you find the Chorus' appearance in the modern-dress production at the National Theatre, London, 2004 (see illustration, p. 14)?

FIRST EPISODE (280–517)
As the Chorus finish their song, the Old Man and Menelaus enter, quarrelling. They are fighting over the letter which Menelaus has intercepted. Agamemnon must have left the stage at the end of the Prologue as the Old Man calls to him in his tent (292).

Stichomythia (280–311)
Stichomythia (single-line dialogue) is a common feature of Greek drama. It offers the chance to alter the pace and intensity of a scene, creates conflict and provides the opportunity to explore the relationship between the two speakers. In this scene the dialogue shifts from the argument between Menelaus and the Old Man to the tense meeting of the brothers Menelaus and Agamemnon.

289 my staff Menelaus is holding a sceptre, a symbol of power, which here he threatens to use as a weapon. He is conscious of his rank, demanding respect (291, 295).

The leader of the white-oared
Fleet of Taphians was Meges, 260
Son of Phyleus,
Who left the islands of Echinades,
Where sailors may not land.

Ajax, reared at Salamis,
Was joining his right wing 265
With the left of those moored
Next to him,
Closing the line
With his twelve most
Manoeuvrable ships. I heard and saw 270
The crew of sailors for myself.
If anyone shall bring his barbarian barge
Near Ajax, there will be
No homecoming for him.
Other things I remember having 275
Heard at home
About the expedition gathered here.
But this is what I saw for myself
Of the fleet of ships.

OLD MAN Menelaus, this is outrageous; you have no right . . . 280
MENELAUS Go away! Your loyalty to your master is too strong.
OLD MAN Is that a reproach? I take it as a compliment.
MENELAUS You'll regret it if you overstep the mark.
OLD MAN You had no business to open the letter I was carrying.
MENELAUS Nor you, to betray all the Greeks. 285
OLD MAN Don't use that argument. Give it back.
MENELAUS I won't.
OLD MAN I'll not let go.
MENELAUS I'll crack your head open with my staff.
OLD MAN Then I'll win glory, dying for my master. 290
MENELAUS Let go! You talk too much, for a slave.

292 Master The Old Man calls to Agamemnon, who is in the tent. Agamemnon replies (294) as he comes out, not at first seeing Menelaus.

297 Look me in the eye! This sharp challenge shows Menelaus' belief that only those with a clear conscience can look one in the eye. His posture, that of someone determined to get to the truth (see 313–14), provokes a powerful response from Agamemnon (298).

301 Not till I've shown the contents Menelaus threatens to breach the secrecy of Agamemnon's dealings. See **'Secrecy and lies'**, p. 12.

311 Smart words are odious The word for smart (*sophos*) is also in the name of the Sophists, freelance teachers of Euripides' day, who were widely thought to subvert morality. The popularity of the rhetorical skills and clever, persuasive techniques of argument which they taught soon led to suspicion about good speakers. See **'Sophistry'**, p. 60.

Agōn (312–88)
The Greeks enjoyed the competitive nature of both legal and political debates. This extended to drama, where we frequently find a pair of confrontational speeches by two characters, called an *agōn* (the Greek word for contest). These were sometimes highly stylised, reflecting the techniques of orators in the assembly and of advocates in court (see 311n and **'Rhetoric 1'**, p. 30).

Friends and enemies 1
The concept of friendship (*philia*) had great importance for the Greeks. Friends (*philoi*) included family and kin, and you were under a moral and social obligation to help your friends at every opportunity. Here Menelaus' reproach, that Agamemnon – having benefited from his friends' help – neglected his duties towards them once he had achieved power (322–7), is a powerful indictment, which most Greeks would have endorsed.

OLD MAN Master, we are wronged. This man has snatched
Your letter from my hand. Agamemnon, he's bent on doing wrong.

AGAMEMNON Hey! What's this commotion at my door, this shouting?

MENELAUS I should be the one to speak, not him. 295

AGAMEMNON You! Menelaus, what's this quarrelling, this violence?

MENELAUS Look me in the eye! Then I'll speak to you.

AGAMEMNON Do you think that I, the son of Atreus, am scared to
look at you?

MENELAUS You see this letter, bearer of the most shameful message?

AGAMEMNON I do. First of all, let go of it. 300

MENELAUS Not till I've shown the contents to all the Greeks.

AGAMEMNON What! You've broken the seal and know
What you had no business to know?

MENELAUS Yes, to your misfortune. I found out your secret plan.

AGAMEMNON Where did you get hold of it? Gods! You have no shame. 305

MENELAUS I was waiting to see if your daughter would come from
Argos to the camp.

AGAMEMNON What right have you to watch over my affairs? Have
you no shame?

MENELAUS I wanted to. I just felt the urge. I am not your slave.

AGAMEMNON This is outrageous. Am I not my own master?

MENELAUS You're devious. Now, before now, always. 310

AGAMEMNON You dress up your wrong. Smart words are odious.

MENELAUS Your mind's unsteady, crooked, not open to your friends.
I'm going to call you to account. Don't get angry
And shrug off the truth. I won't be too hard on you.
You remember when you set your heart 315
On being the Greek leader against Troy,
Wanting not to seem to want it, but really craving it –
How modest you were, offering your hand to everyone,
Your door open to anyone, greeting one and all,
Willy, nilly, seeking in this way 320
To buy yourself distinction, by general consent?
Then, when you achieved your office, you changed your ways,
Were friend no longer to your former friends,
Aloof and rarely seen, behind closed doors.

342 under no constraint Menelaus anticipates that Agamemnon will claim (as in lines 98–100) that Menelaus had urged him to send the letter to Clytaemnestra. Menelaus is silent about his part in the decision, leaving us uncertain about who is telling the truth.

The Greek states

Greece was not a unified country in ancient times, but a collection of individual city states (*poleis*) which had their own rulers and laws. The only expression of an overall Greek identity was the common language and the festivals of Olympia, Delphi, Isthmia and Nemea, which were open to all the states. The expedition to Troy was the first time that the states joined together to fight a common enemy (329, 397). In 490–479 BC they again successfully presented a unified front against a common enemy, the Persians. The alliance, however, soon broke up, largely because of the growing power and imperial ambitions of Athens, and in 431 BC the Greek world was plunged into a bitter internal conflict, the Peloponnesian War, between two groups of states, led by Athens and Sparta. This play, first performed (*c.* 405 BC) when Athens was about to suffer humiliating defeat at the hands of other Greeks, takes the minds of its first audience away from their dire plight to a world in which the Greeks are united against barbarians (285, 329, 353).

354 Those barbarian nobodies Here Menelaus is speaking about the Trojans, but the Greek audience would possibly be thinking also of the Persians (see **'Barbarians and Troy'**, p. 8).

355 Because of you and your daughter Agamemnon has many responsibilities: to the army of the Greeks, as their commander; to those who swore Tyndareus' oath; to his friends and supporters (323); and to his whole family, including Menelaus and his own wife and children. By juxtaposing the 'noble mission' of the Greeks and 'your daughter', in an emotive way Menelaus simplifies Agamemnon's dilemma, implying that a father's love for his child cannot stand in the way of a campaign in which the honour of all Greece is at stake (354).

Leadership 1

Menelaus presents a view of leadership different from that of the Homeric world, in which princes led their contingents. The picture which Menelaus gives of Agamemnon's pursuit of office – with the implication that he was elected (315–21, 349–50) – resembles that of the Athens of Euripides' day. Though many of the offices of state were chosen by lot, the generals (*strategoi*) were elected.

A good man engaged in a great enterprise   325
Should not change his ways, but be steadfast with his friends
Especially when, by prospering, he can most help them.
This was when I first found fault with you, when I first realised
     your weakness.
When you then came to Aulis with the army of All Greece,
You were reduced to nothing. You were confounded   330
By the fate the gods had dealt you,
With no wind for the crossing.
The Greek talk was for disbanding the fleet,
Not toiling for nothing in Aulis.
You seemed ill-fated, doomed, if, with your thousand ships,   335
You could not invade Priam's kingdom.
You called me in. 'What can I do? How find a way
Of not losing my command and my prestige?'
Then, when Calchas said you should offer your daughter
As a sacrifice to Artemis so that the Greeks could sail,   340
You were delighted and cheerfully offered to sacrifice
Your child. Of your own accord, under no constraint –
Don't claim that! – you sent word to your wife
To send your daughter here, under pretext
Of marrying Achilles. And then you wriggled out of it   345
And you've been caught sending a second message.
So, you can't murder your own daughter? Yes, you can.
This is the self-same air that heard you the first time.
Countless men have had the same experience. They struggle
To power, only to have a miserable fall, sometimes   350
Because of the public's ignorance, sometimes deservedly,
Because they do not have the ability to safeguard the state.
It's Greece that I pity. She embarked on a noble mission, but now
Those barbarian nobodies are let off the hook, to laugh at her,
Because of you and your daughter.   355

Leadership 2

Menelaus suggests that the main quality of a general should be intelligence and not just bravery (357). The idea may have suggested to the first audience incidents in the Peloponnesian War, including the disaster for Athens of the Sicilian expedition of 415–413 BC. The Athenians had been persuaded to undertake the expedition by their most gifted general, Alcibiades. On the eve of the expedition religious statues in Athens were desecrated but, despite the bad omen, the Athenians decided to sail. Alcibiades, however, was recalled to Athens to face charges of impiety and their forces, led by an unimaginative general, Nicias, were defeated by the superior strategy of the Spartans.

Menelaus' speech

- How does Menelaus' version of events differ from that which Agamemnon has given us? Have we any means of knowing which is more credible?
- What impression do we get of Menelaus?

Honour and reputation

The Greeks prized honour (Greek *timē*) highly. Noble men and women should in their religious, civic and moral practice aim at the highest standards. A man's honour won respect and a good reputation, which reflected both on him and on his family and country. To be dishonourable or cowardly brought disgrace and public shame. Agamemnon, who has felt the sting of Menelaus' reproaches, is quick to assert that he knows the difference between honourable and shameful conduct (362–4).

370 It isn't my position which gnaws at you Agamemnon responds in kind to his brother's taunts above (312–58). He presents Menelaus as a cuckold, pining to recover his unfaithful wife (367–76).

Changing one's mind 1

Until this point, changing one's mind has been presented as a sign of instability or weakness (34–41, 312, 345). Agamemnon (374) challenges this view: to change a misguided decision is simply good sense.

The suitors' oath

A characteristic of the play is differing versions of events. Agamemnon says that the suitors swore Tyndareus' oath (59) because they hoped to win Helen's hand in marriage, not because they wanted to help Menelaus (378). Their lust (377) acted as a form of duress (383) and so rendered the oath non-binding. This means that Menelaus has no claim on the loyalty of the other Greeks and he can't dress up his desire to recover Helen as a duty to Greece. His vision of a Panhellenic mission collapses (355n).

I wouldn't have anyone lead his country or an army
Just because of his courage. It's intelligence a country's general needs.
Anyone can do it, if he has the brains.

CHORUS It's bad for brothers to fall to insults and to quarrelling
When they disagree.   360

AGAMEMNON It's my turn now to criticise you. I intend to be brief,
Not letting my sight stray beyond what honour demands.
I'll show restraint: you are my brother.
A man of honour knows where to draw the line.
Tell me: what's the meaning of these threats and bluster,   365
These bloodshot eyes? Who is wronging you? What do you want?
Is it a faithful wife you long for? I can't help you.
The one you had, you could not control. Am I to pay
For your misfortunes? I have done nothing wrong.
It isn't my position which gnaws at you. You long   370
For that specious wife in your arms, with no regard
For reason or for honour. The pleasures of a worthless man
Resemble him – they're sordid. If I made a wrong decision,
Then saw sense and changed my mind, am I mad?
You are the madman to want your wife back: 375
God gave you the good fortune to lose her.
The suitors swore Tyndareus' oath – misguided, lustful men;
It was more to do with hope – or some god – than with you
And your influence. Well, take them and go to war.
In their stupidity they are prepared for it.   380
It's not hard to know what the gods approve;
One can tell the difference between oaths badly phrased and those
Made under duress. I will not kill my own child.
You won't settle your score with your unworthy wife by ways
Which are not just, leaving me to wear out days and nights in tears, 385
Defying justice and the law in my treatment of my children.
That's all I have to say: brief, clear, not hard to understand.
You may choose folly; I'll arrange my own affairs as is right.

CHORUS This is not what he said before. But I'm glad
That he will spare his child.   390

Friends and enemies 2

391 So, I have no longer family or friends? Agamemnon has implied that the suitors were not Menelaus' true friends (see **'The suitors' oath'**, p. 28); and Menelaus feels betrayed by Agamemnon (393, 399), who says he does not fully support his brother (396).

Panhellenism v. family loyalty

In a last bid for Agamemnon's support Menelaus appeals first to his brother's love (395); when that fails, he again appeals to his sense of patriotic duty (397, 355n). But Agamemnon now is standing firm, insisting that, in refusing to kill his daughter, he has justice and the law on his side (386).

398 It is some god's doing When Greeks attribute control over their lives to the gods, they are often referring to fortune or fate (33, 331, 376, 378, 423) or some strong passion (70n, 773) – accounting for what it is otherwise hard to explain. This way of speaking in Euripides' day did not necessarily imply literal belief.

399 Vaunt your general's staff See 289n.

Rhetoric 1

Greek society prized the art of speaking. Rhetoric was formally taught, and was employed not only in law-courts and political debates, but also in the theatre. Rhetorical skills focused upon the structure of speeches (balancing, contrasting, numbering points and arguments; repetition of words; working up to an emotional ending) and on the introduction of variety and 'drama' by means of pathos, exclamations, imaginary debate, the use of rhetorical questions or addressing oneself to someone absent.

- What is the tone of Agamemnon's speech (361–88)?
- How does he answer Menelaus' charge? How convincing is his argument?
- At the end of the *agōn* whose case is the more compelling? Does the exchange feel more like a formalised debate or a realistic quarrel between two brothers?

Entry of first Messenger

Menelaus' threat suggests that he is about to leave the stage, but he is stopped by the entry of Messenger 1 (401). The entry of a new character in tragedy was often announced by a character on stage. For someone to enter so abruptly, interrupting another speaker (here in the middle of a line), is very unusual – and also difficult on the wide, open Greek stage. Like the similarly unexpected entry of Menelaus and the Old Man (280), this marks a sudden turn in events and creates dramatic tension.

MENELAUS So, I have no longer family or friends?

AGAMEMNON Of course you have, unless you want to destroy them.

MENELAUS Can you convince me that you're my brother?

AGAMEMNON I want us to see sense together, not share some sickness.

MENELAUS We should share the pain of those close to us.   395

AGAMEMNON You can call on me if you treat me well, not if you
    cause me grief.

MENELAUS Don't you see that Greece shares your grief?

AGAMEMNON Greece shares your sickness. It is some god's doing.

MENELAUS Vaunt your general's staff. You have betrayed your brother.
    But I'll find other ways and other friends.   400

MESSENGER 1 Agamemnon, commander of all the Greeks,
    I have brought your daughter, Iphigeneia.
    Her mother Clytaemnestra is with her
    And your son, Orestes, whom you'll be pleased to see,
    Having been so long away from home.   405
    They've had a long journey, so they are cooling their feet
    By a shallow stream. We've let the horses
    On to a lush meadow, to graze.

*Menelaus and Agamemnon (National
Theatre, London, 2004).*

409 The army knows Agamemnon's attempts to conceal his plans are now defeated. Menelaus' threat to reveal all to the army (301) is about to be realised: news of the wedding plan is breaking and the crowd becomes a player in the action.

Greek marriage customs

Before a young Greek girl was married, certain ceremonies and rites were performed. First she would offer up her toys and clothes to the gods; this marked the transition from her role as girl to that of wife. Sacrifices to Artemis in her capacity as goddess of virginity were also made; it was thought that this would help ease the transition to married life (416ff). Barley was sprinkled on a sacrificial victim before it was killed, and the animal would be decorated with garlands (419). (See **'Sacrifice'**, p. 46.) At the wedding feast, songs of male and female choruses played an integral part, a symbol of the new male/female relationship embodied in the wedding; and there would be dancing (420–1).

416 They're consecrating the girl to Artemis There is a grim, unintentional ambiguity in this phrase. The ritual of sacrifice to Artemis preceded marriage (see **'Greek marriage customs'** above), but the sacrifice which the audience is thinking of is that of Iphigeneia herself.

422 Do go inside The Messenger enters the tent. Menelaus and the Chorus remain, but Agamemnon seems to ignore their presence.

425 the yoke of necessity This term recalls words in Aeschylus' *Agamemnon*, when the Chorus describe the same dilemma. Agamemnon, knowing that whatever he does, he will do wrong, 'buckled on the harness of necessity'.

426 Some spirit has appeared The Greeks had separate words for a god (*theos*, 378, 398) and a spirit (*daimōn*). A *daimōn* tends to attach itself to an individual, often to affect their fate adversely.

436 arriving uninvited The letter (100–1) told Clytaemnestra to send Iphigeneia to Aulis. Agamemnon suggests he did not invite his wife to accompany her. Even so, her arrival for her daughter's wedding is entirely understandable.

440 Hades will soon have her, I think, as his bride An unmarried girl who died was often considered to have 'married death', to have moved to the house of Hades, god of the underworld. Antigone in Sophocles' *Antigone* becomes a bride of Hades, as does Polyxena in Euripides' *Hecuba*.

442–3 may your own marriage / Prove like mine Agamemnon imagines what Iphigeneia will say to him in vivid direct speech. The words, full of pathos, ironically foreshadow his own fate (see **'Clytaemnestra 2'**, p. 78).

I've come ahead to prepare you. The army knows –
The rumour's raced ahead – your daughter has arrived.   410
A whole crowd is rushing here to catch sight of her.
The great and good are celebrated. People want to see them.
They're saying, 'Is there a wedding? What's happening?
Or has Agamemnon brought his daughter here because
He's missing her?' But you could hear from others   415
'They're consecrating the girl to Artemis, the queen of Aulis,
Before her marriage. Who do you think will be the groom?'
If that's the case, come on, make a start, with baskets
Of barley and garlands for the head. And, Menelaus,
Prepare the wedding song. Let's hear the sound of flute   420
And dancing inside!

AGAMEMNON Thank you. Do go inside.
If fortune is kind, all will be well.
Oh, what can I say? Where can I begin?
We've slipped into the yoke of necessity.   425
Some spirit has appeared, far cleverer than my stratagems.
Low birth has its advantages: *they* find it easy
To weep and talk about their troubles, whereas
Nobles have nothing but misfortune. Our life
Is ruled by pride, we are the slaves of the mob.   430
I am ashamed to weep, but not to weep
Is also shameful in this terrible predicament.
So . . . what shall I say to my wife? How can I
Receive her? How compose my face?
She has destroyed me – on top of the existing   435
Troubles – by arriving uninvited. But it's understandable
That she should come, to marry off her daughter and
Give her blessings – and then she will discover
My treachery. As for the poor maid – why 'maid'?
Hades will soon have her, I think, as his bride.   440
I pity her. I can imagine her pleading 'Father,
Are you going to kill me? Then may your own marriage
Prove like mine, yours, your family's and friends'!'

Agamemnon confounded

Agamemnon seemed to have gathered strength in his altercation with his brother, but the Messenger's news leaves him devastated. He finds it hard to focus his thoughts (424), is plunged again into envy of the common man (427–8), and blames some spirit (426), necessity (425), his pride and the mob (430). Here it is the common man's freedom to express emotion openly which he envies (it was freedom from danger before, 17–27, 87). He weeps (431; see 456, 473 and 39) – which would be thought unmanly, if done in public. He feels powerless, a slave – to necessity (425) and to the mob (430, see also **'The army'**, p. 36). His secret plotting is now revealed. The news of Clytaemnestra's imminent arrival is the crowning misfortune (436–7), pitching him into despair (435, 447).

- Why will Clytaemnestra's arrival have the effect of 'the yoke of necessity'?
- Is it clear whether Agamemnon will now sacrifice his daughter?
○ Does Agamemnon (422–47) seem to be speaking to himself or does he address Menelaus?

450 Brother, give me your hand! Menelaus has been silent through the previous scene. This powerful gesture of reconciliation introduces another totally unexpected twist in the story.

451 I give way to you The words could even mean 'I cede power to you.'

452–3 Pelops . . . Atreus See **'House of Pelops'**, p. 36, and **'Ancestry'**, p. 68.

474 the prophecy Menelaus assures Agamemnon that, as far as he is concerned, Calchas' prophecy is no impediment to his sparing Iphigeneia. There seems to be no fear of divine retribution if the sacrifice is not made.

Changing one's mind 2

Menelaus now justifies *his* change of mind (477, see 393): he has been overwhelmed by his emotions, his love for his brother and the realisation of what it means to kill a child (467). He is determined to prevent the death not only of Iphigeneia, but also of his own daughter by Helen, Hermione (460). Family loyalty has triumphed; the expedition to Troy can be abandoned (472).

- How convincing is Menelaus' change of mind?

And Orestes will be there. He can't talk yet,
He'll make his baby sounds, but he will understand.　　445
Oh! It is Paris, son of Priam, who has brought this about.
He has destroyed me, by his marriage with Helen.
CHORUS I pity you. Though a stranger,
　　I am a woman and must lament a ruler's troubles.
MENELAUS Brother, give me your hand!　　450
AGAMEMNON I do. I give way to you. I am so wretched.
MENELAUS I swear by Pelops, the father of my father
　　And of yours, and by Atreus, who gave us birth,
　　I'll tell you straight what's in my heart:
　　Not what suits me, but what I really feel.　　455
　　When I saw you weeping, I pitied you and shed a tear
　　Myself. I take back my former words, with no
　　Ill-feeling against you. I put myself in your position.
　　My advice is: do not kill your child and do not take
　　Mine in her place. It is not right that you　　460
　　Should grieve at my expense, that your child should die
　　While mine enjoys life. What do I want? A wife?
　　I could make another excellent marriage, if that's what I want.
　　Shall I destroy my brother – the last person I should –
　　And choose Helen, evil in place of good?　　465
　　I was stupid and naive, until I looked at the situation
　　Closely and realised what it means to kill a child.
　　Besides, I was overcome with pity for the poor girl
　　As I realised it was my own niece who was going to
　　Be sacrificed, for the sake of my marriage.　　470
　　What has your daughter to do with Helen?
　　Disband the army, let them leave Aulis.
　　And, brother, stop this outpouring of tears
　　And stop provoking mine! As for the prophecy about your
　　　　daughter,
　　Be sure I want no part in it: I leave that to you.　　475
　　Do I revoke all my harsh words? I do, and rightly.
　　My love for my brother has changed me. It's not
　　A sign of weakness, to follow the best of motives.

House of Pelops

The history of Agamemnon's family is fraught with crime and murder, cursed ever since their ancestor **Tantalus** (479) served his son's flesh to the gods. His son **Pelops** (452) won his wife Hippodameia by treachery and violence, passing on blood-guilt to his sons, Atreus and Thyestes. Their feud over the throne of Argos led to **Atreus** (453) serving Thyestes a meal of Thyestes' own children. Thyestes invoked a curse on Atreus and his family – his sons Agamemnon and Menelaus. The feud was continued through Thyestes' son Aegisthus, who became Clytaemnestra's lover when Agamemnon went to Troy.

480 You do not shame your ancestry See 'Ancestry', p. 68.

486 no option but / The bloody murder See **'Agamemnon confounded'**, p. 34.

● Does this change of mind surprise you? How long might we have suspected it?

The army

So far the army has been the object of the Chorus' admiration or shown excitedly speculating about a wedding. We are now given a different picture, of a powerful mob susceptible to the lead of a corrupt priest and the ambitious, unscrupulous Odysseus. This threat to his authority perhaps explains Agamemnon's insecurity; it has, maybe, been preying on him since the Prologue (18–23, 87), making him feel the slave 'of the mob' (430), fearful of their power to destroy him and his city (507–10). Now his duplicity is about to become public knowledge.

This army differs from that in Homer's epics, which is removed from the action as the focus is upon individual heroes. The picture reflects the power and volatility of the crowd in late fifth-century democratic Greece. At Athens the citizen assembly was swayed by demagogues into votes of vicious retribution on recalcitrant allies or of execution for generals who failed in their duty (as after the Battle of Arginusae, 406 BC).

493 Calchas will reveal the oracle Calchas' oracle was known only by Odysseus, Menelaus and Agamemnon (see 504 and **'Secrecy and lies'**, p. 12).

494 Not if he's killed in time The idea of murdering the priest Calchas makes Menelaus a credible descendant of his family (479). It introduces an unexpectedly sinister, melodramatic turn in the story.

495 ambitious priests There are other plays in which characters accuse priests of corruption and ambition (Pentheus in *Bacchae*; Creon in *Antigone*).

CHORUS Noble words and worthy of Tantalus, the son
Of Zeus. You do not shame your ancestry.   480

AGAMEMNON I admire you, Menelaus. Your offer goes
Beyond my expectation. It's right and worthy of you.
Discord between brothers is caused by sex
And greed within a family. I loathe
Such bitterness within the family.   485
Yet our situation leaves us no option but
The bloody murder of my daughter.

MENELAUS Why? Who will compel you to kill her?

AGAMEMNON The whole army of the Greeks, gathered here.

MENELAUS Not if you send her back to Argos.   490

AGAMEMNON I could do that, unnoticed; but there's something
else I can't hide.

MENELAUS What? Don't be too scared of the mob.

AGAMEMNON Calchas will reveal the oracle to the Greek army.

MENELAUS Not if he's killed in time. It will be easy.

AGAMEMNON The whole breed of ambitious priests is corrupt.   495

MENELAUS Corrupt and useless.

Odysseus

In the *Iliad* Odysseus is a brave and enterprising fighter at Troy; in the *Odyssey*, as the hero whose protracted journey home from Troy is the theme of the poem, he manifests the qualities of a survivor, not least courage and ingenuity: the trick by which he and his companions escaped from the monstrous Cyclops (book 9) is a good example of his cunning. The Greek playwrights felt free to adapt the characters of their protagonists. Odysseus sometimes, as in Sophocles' *Ajax*, is a sympathetic character, but he is more often presented as cunning and a plausible liar. Here (501) the portrayal of Odysseus resembles the demagogues in fifth-century BC Athens. They were clever but unprincipled speakers who roused the mob into supporting them. They are wonderfully ridiculed in Aristophanes' comedy *The Knights*.

509–10 plunder the region and raze / The city Such behaviour is untypical of soldiers in the *Iliad* and of those of Euripides' day. The picture, expressed by Agamemnon, of the power of an unruly mob, led by unprincipled leaders, is probably suggested by the behaviour of the citizen body in the assembly (see **'The army'**, p. 36).

517 say nothing The Chorus remain in the *orchēstra* throughout the play. They cannot be ignored. Because they have heard his plan, Agamemnon must ask them to say nothing to Clytaemnestra. Medea in Euripides' *Medea* similarly swears the Chorus to secrecy about her plans for revenge on her husband.

Agamemnon and Necessity 1

Agamemnon says that the gods leave him no way out (511–12). He blames 'Some spirit' (426) and the gods (511–12), but he is not to be taken literally (398n). Piety requires that he perform the sacrifice (see **'Demands of religion'**, p. 4), but his sense of being powerless seems to have more to do with the hostility and power of Odysseus (501–11) and the menace of the troops (430, 509–11) than with fear of the gods. There is no suggestion that Agamemnon tries to resist the pressure and stand up for his own moral principles, as Antigone, for example, does in Sophocles' *Antigone*.

- Is Agamemnon the victim of necessity? To what extent is his behaviour determined by his own moral weakness?

AGAMEMNON Are you afraid of what I'm thinking?

MENELAUS How can I know, if you don't tell me?

AGAMEMNON Odysseus knows all this.

MENELAUS Odysseus won't harm us.   500

AGAMEMNON He's cunning, always siding with the mob.

MENELAUS He certainly has the curse of ambition.

AGAMEMNON Can't you imagine him, surrounded by
    The Greeks, revealing the oracle which Calchas announced?
    He'll say that I first undertook the sacrifice to Artemis   505
    And then proved false. He'll seize control of the troops
    And order the Argives to murder you and me and then
    To sacrifice the girl. And if I escape to Argos,
    They'll come and plunder the region and raze
    The city to the ground, Cyclopean walls and all.   510
    That's what I would face. The gods leave me
    With no way out. Do one thing for me, Menelaus;
    As you go through the army, take care that Clytaemnestra
    Does not find out what's happening – until I have
    Taken my child and committed her to Hades.   515
    So I can do my wretched task with the minimum of tears.
    And you, foreign ladies, say nothing.

FIRST CHORAL ODE (FIRST *STASIMON*) (518–81)

A *stasimon* is a formal ode, which was sung by the chorus as they danced in the *orchēstra* (see *Introduction to the Greek Theatre*, pp. 112–15). The theme is often suggested by the preceding episode and may also serve as a link with the next. Agamemnon and Menelaus leave the stage separately. The Chorus in two matching stanzas sing about sexual desire and the importance, for individual happiness and for the state (549), of modesty and self-restraint. In the epode (550–66) they reveal the relevance of these musings: Agamemnon has cursed the marriage of Paris and Helen (447). Their mutual love, uncontrolled passion at first sight (559–63, 75), has brought their countries to the brink of war.

Moderation

So fearful were ordinary Greeks of excess (519), of going beyond their natural and rightful lot and thereby angering the gods, that they recommended moderation (*sōphrosynē*) in all aspects of life. Aphrodite, the goddess of love, has us all potentially in her power. In other plays of Euripides a female chorus treat sexual passion as frightening and dangerous: in *Medea* Jason's adultery causes his wife, Medea, to murder their children; in *Hippolytus* Phaedra's passion for her step-son, induced by Aphrodite, leads her to suicide.

524 Eros An ancient deity who represents the power of sexual passion, originally depicted as a handsome athlete. Gradually he became associated with Aphrodite, as her companion or son.

530 Fairest queen of Cyprus See 175n.

538 the ways we bring our children up The relative importance of nature and nurture is a common topic in the thought of Euripides' day. Here there is no debate: each seems to complement the other.

CHORUS Happiness belongs to those
Who have without excess
Known the delights of Aphrodite,   520
When the goddess is in gentle mood,
Avoiding the turbulence
Of frenzied lust.
Golden-haired Eros has two bows
To shoot his favours –   525
One bestows a life of bliss,
The other ruin.
The second I will not admit
Within our bedroom,
Fairest queen of Cyprus.   530
May my joy be temperate,
My desires pure,
Let me know the joy of sex,
But not its tyranny.

The nature of mortals is varied   535
And varied are their ways,
But straightforward virtue is plain.
And the ways we bring our children up
Affect their virtue greatly.
Wisdom lies in moderation.   540
It has the pre-eminent grace
Of knowing what is right.
And its reputation brings
Undying fame to men.
It is important that we pursue virtue –   545
Women through the modesty of their love;
And among men too inner self-control,
Multiplied a thousandfold,
Will make a country great.

550–2 Paris ... a herdsman ... on Ida See 77n.

553 native tunes Herdsmen traditionally played pipes while out with their cattle or goats. In the theatre the chorus' songs were also accompanied by a pipe.

Clytaemnestra's arrival

As the Chorus finish their formal ode, Clytaemnestra and her party arrive. As their carriage (576) makes its way to the centre of the stage, the entry could be both spectacular and fraught with suspense. The Chorus, sworn to secrecy about Agamemnon's plans (517), fall into an obsequious and effusive greeting (567–81).

568 my Lady Iphigeneia Lines 567–81 could be spoken by a secondary chorus, entering with Clytaemnestra, presumably her attendants. This is not unheard of in tragedy (e.g. *Hippolytus*) but not necessary here.

○ How might a producer use an extra chorus to add to the effect of this scene?

SECOND EPISODE (582–726)
Clytaemnestra 1

The figure of Clytaemnestra was familiar in Greek literature as early as Homer. In the *Odyssey* she is known as the murderer of her husband on his return from the Trojan War. In Aeschylus' *Agamemnon* she plots and then carries out his murder. Subsequently, she appears in Sophocles' *Electra* and Euripides' *Electra* and *Orestes*, where she is presented less as a villain and more as a victim of her own emotions and of her new husband Aegisthus (see **'House of Pelops'**, p. 36).

You have gone back, Paris, to where   550
You were raised, a herdsman
Where white heifers graze on Ida;
Playing your native tunes
You breathed from your pipe sounds
To match the music of the gods.   555
Laden with milk the cattle grazed
As you judged the contest of the goddesses,
Which brought you to Greece.
And as you stood before the throne of Sparta,
Ivory-inlaid, you looked   560
Straight into the eyes of Helen
And you offered love and felt,
Within yourself, the thrill of love.
Now cry 'War! War!'
As you provoke the ships and armament of Greece   565
Against the citadel of Troy.

Io! Blessings on the great!
Look, here come my Lady Iphigeneia,
The king's daughter, and Clytaemnestra,
Daughter of Tyndareus.   570
From great ancestry they are sprung
And they have come to great prosperity.
Our lords and benefactors are gods
To less fortunate mortals.

Women of Chalchis, let's stand here   575
And help the queen down from her carriage.
Don't let her stumble. Gently with your hands.
Take care that Agamemnon's splendid child
Should not take fright on her arrival,
And that we strangers cause no disturbance   580
To alarm the Argive ladies.

CLYTAEMNESTRA I take this as an auspicious omen –
Your courtesy and your kindly words.

584–5 I am here / To lead my daughter We are left in no doubt that Clytaemnestra has received Agamemnon's first letter telling her to bring Iphigeneia for her betrothal to Achilles (600–1).

Stage business
Clytaemnestra gives orders to a series of attendants 586–95 – or possibly to members of the Chorus (see 577–81).

586 the dowry See 'Marriage and dowries', p. 6.

601 The son of a Nereid See 226n, 675.

Dramatic irony
Agamemnon, after re-entering the stage (by 606), stands for a while silent. The audience's awareness of his plan to sacrifice Iphigeneia – and Clytaemnestra and her daughter's ignorance – give the scene a special poignancy (616–50).

Iphigeneia in Agamemnon's arms (Crucible Theatre, Sheffield, 2002).

It gives me hope that I am here
To lead my daughter to a noble marriage.   585
Take from my carriage the dowry which I bring
For her and carry it with care inside.
My child, leave the carriage,
Mind your foot, so delicate and frail.
Girls, support her on your arms,   590
Help her out. Someone offer me an arm,
To help me from my seat with dignity.
And you! Stand in front of the horses:
Their look can be frightening and pitiless.
Take the baby, Agamemnon's son, Orestes.   595
He doesn't talk yet. My child, are you asleep,
Lulled by the rocking of the coach?
Wake up! It is your sister's wedding!
Bring her luck! You are a noble child
And you shall have a noble brother-in-law,   600
The son of a Nereid, half-divine.
Sit here, at my feet, my baby.
And, Iphigeneia, make your mother happy:
Stand there beside the foreign ladies
And greet your dear father.   605
Your majesty, my lord, Agamemnon, we have arrived
In response to your command.

IPHIGENEIA Mother, don't be angry, if I'm first
To hug my father. I've wanted for so long,
Father, to run and take you in my arms!   610
I've missed you! Don't be cross!

CLYTAEMNESTRA Of course you must! You've always
Loved your father most of all my children.

IPHIGENEIA Father, I'm so happy to see you after all this time.

AGAMEMNON And I to see you. You speak for both of us.   615

IPHIGENEIA Hello. You did well to send for me.

AGAMEMNON I'm not sure I can say that, my child.

IPHIGENEIA Oh dear! You look anxious, for one who's happy to see me.

AGAMEMNON A king and a general has many cares.

627 the Phrygians Troy was in Phrygia, in the west of Asia Minor (see map, p. vii).

644 You're not sending me to live in someone else's home? The question reveals Iphigeneia's naivety. We do not know her age, but Greek girls were betrothed very young.

Sacrifice

Animal sacrifice was a common element of ritual, to express thanks to the gods or ask for their favour. An animal, usually domesticated and preferably spotless, was sprinkled with corn and wine or water, garlanded and led – it must appear, willingly – to an altar in front of a temple or in the home. When killed, its blood was collected and poured on the ground, the edible parts were cooked and shared by those present and other parts (mainly the thigh bones and fat) burnt for the enjoyment of the gods.

652 A young girl should not be seen here In Greek society it was considered improper and shameful for young women to be seen out of doors without a chaperone. Although Iphigeneia is accompanied by her mother, the male world of an army camp is no place for any woman.

Parent–child relationships

We see here not only the parental concern which Clytaemnestra shows towards her daughter and baby son (589–98), but also the touching relationship between father and daughter. Her spontaneous affection is natural and uninhibited. The *stichomythia* allows the reunion to be emotionally charged and the dramatic irony to develop at pace. The tenderness of the parting (654–8) is heightened by the irony and the setting – the family group, including the baby, in the army camp.

Domestic drama

This scene focuses more on domestic detail than was usual in tragedy, and in other ways too our play has features associated with the later theatrical genre known as New Comedy. Once Sophocles and Euripides were dead, tragedy was succeeded by a more melodramatic and sentimental style of drama that has survived largely in fragmentary form, but we do have one complete play, *Dyscolos* (*Bad-tempered Man*) by Menander. The plays do not deal in large moral issues or in the political and social satire of the Old Comedy of Aristophanes, but rather with the private life of a well-to-do family. In this scene the dialogue between Agamemnon and Clytaemnestra about the proposed marriage and their future son-in-law has a natural, conversational tone and the *stichomythia* facilitates the escalating friction between the two.

IPHIGENEIA You're with me now – forget your worries.   620

AGAMEMNON I'm with you wholly. Nowhere else.

IPHIGENEIA Then stop frowning. Smile!

AGAMEMNON I'm happy, as I always am to see you.

IPHIGENEIA But you're crying!

AGAMEMNON We're going to be parted for a long time.   625

IPHIGENEIA I don't know what you're saying. Dearest father,
    I don't understand. Where do they say the Phrygians live?

AGAMEMNON Where Priam's son Paris should never have lived.

IPHIGENEIA You'll leave me and go far away, father.

AGAMEMNON You will end in the same place as your father.   630
    You seem to understand. That makes me sadder.

IPHIGENEIA Then I'll talk nonsense, if that will cheer you up.

AGAMEMNON Thank you. Oh, I don't have the strength to keep silent.

IPHIGENEIA Stay at home, father, with your children.

AGAMEMNON I'd like to, but I can't. That's what upsets me.   635

IPHIGENEIA Damn the army and Menelaus' troubles.

AGAMEMNON What's damned me will damn others.

IPHIGENEIA You've been away a long time at Aulis.

AGAMEMNON Something prevents me launching the expedition.

IPHIGENEIA I wish you could take me with you.   640

AGAMEMNON You will make a journey and you won't forget your father.

IPHIGENEIA With my mother? Or shall I go alone?

AGAMEMNON Alone, without your father or your mother.

IPHIGENEIA You're not sending me to live in someone else's home?

AGAMEMNON Stop. Young girls should not know things like that.   645

IPHIGENEIA Hurry back from Phrygia, father, when you've done
    your work there.

AGAMEMNON First I have to make a sacrifice here.

IPHIGENEIA You must do what's right and make a sacrifice.

AGAMEMNON You will know. You'll stand by the holy water.

IPHIGENEIA Shall we have dancing round the altar?   650

AGAMEMNON How I envy you your innocence.
    Now go inside. A young girl should not be seen here.
    First give me a kiss and hold my hand.

671 Aegina . . . Asopus Aegina was the daughter of the river god Asopus. The river flows through Boeotia in central Greece. Aegina was kidnapped by Zeus and her father pursued them, but was driven off by Zeus' thunderbolts. Zeus carried her to the island of Oinone (673) off Attica, which thereafter bore her name. There she gave birth to a son, Aeacus.

673 Aeacus Aeacus ruled the island named after his mother, which suffered from a terrible plague. With most of the island's inhabitants dead, he asked his father Zeus to repopulate his kingdom. Zeus did so by changing ants into people called Myrmidons ('ant-people'). There is a tradition that Aeacus' sons Telamon and Peleus killed their half-brother Phocus, for which their father banished them. This is why the followers of Peleus, who went to Thessaly, are called Myrmidons.

The marriage of Peleus and Thetis

Zeus, who was anxious to avoid the fate which marriage to Thetis entailed (see *Background to the story*, p. v), took over the role – which her father would normally have had – of giving her away (677). Zeus' involvement also explains the lavish celebrations (681), which are described in the third choral ode (995ff).

679 Cheiron A Centaur (half-man, half-horse). Unlike his wild race, he was kind, just and wise, skilled especially in medicine and music. Living in a cave on Mount Pelion, he was tutor to Asclepius, god of medicine, and the hero Jason, as well as Achilles (see also 891).

Agamemnon and Clytaemnestra (from Cacoyannis' film Ifigeneia, *1977).*

You're going to be parted from your father
For a long time. Dear heart! Your cheeks . . .   655
Your golden hair . . . What a grief Troy and Helen
Have become for us. I'll say no more. As soon
As I touch you, I am overcome by tears. Go in!
Forgive me, daughter of Leda, if I'm too distressed
At giving my daughter away to Achilles.   660
Such parting can bring blessings, but it can
Be hard for parents when a father under stress
Parts with his children to another home.

CLYTAEMNESTRA I understand. I too shall feel the same –
So I'll not reproach you – when I lead   665
Our daughter into marriage.
But custom and time will make less the pain.
Now, I know the name of the man
You've promised our daughter to; I want
To know about his family and where he's from.   670

AGAMEMNON Aegina was the daughter of Asopus . . .

CLYTAEMNESTRA Who was her husband? A god or mortal?

AGAMEMNON Zeus. She bore Aeacus, the lord of Oinone.

CLYTAEMNESTRA And who was Aeacus' heir?

AGAMEMNON Peleus. And Peleus married a daughter of Nereus.   675

CLYTAEMNESTRA Did he take her with the god's consent, or by force?

AGAMEMNON Zeus betrothed her, and with his authority gave her away.

CLYTAEMNESTRA Where did he marry her? Beneath the sea?

AGAMEMNON Where Cheiron lives, on the holy range of Pelion.

CLYTAEMNESTRA Where they say the race of Centaurs lives?   680

AGAMEMNON Yes, that's where the gods gave Peleus his wedding feast.

CLYTAEMNESTRA Was it Thetis who brought up Achilles or his father?

AGAMEMNON Cheiron, so that he didn't learn the ways of wicked mortals.

CLYTAEMNESTRA So he had a wise tutor; and a wise father to arrange this.

AGAMEMNON That's the man who'll be our child's husband.   685

CLYTAEMNESTRA I can't find fault. Where in Greece does he live?

AGAMEMNON By the river Apidanus, in the land of Phthia.

CLYTAEMNESTRA Is that where he'll take your daughter and mine?

AGAMEMNON It is for him to decide, when she is his.

692 the preliminary sacrifice to the goddess See 'Greek marriage customs', p. 32.

The setting of the army camp

We are reminded again that women are most out of place in the army's camp. Clytaemnestra is not sure it is a suitable place for the women's feast (698) and it is Agamemnon's argument in urging her to go back home (709). See 652n.

The mother of the bride

In addition to the sacrifice (692) and feast for the women (696), we have more glimpses of Greek wedding customs. The mother of the bride played an important part, as revealed by Clytaemnestra's shock when she hears that the wedding is to go ahead without her (702–10, see 665–6). The bride was escorted to her husband's house by a torch-lit procession (706).

714 the goddess queen of Argos Hera, the patron goddess of Argos and goddess of marriage.

Respect for the gods

When Agamemnon's plan to remove Clytaemnestra from the sacrifice is foiled (718–19), he turns once more to the soothsayer Calchas (722). Just as Clytaemnestra is concerned about ritual correctness (698, 708), Agamemnon needs to be seen to consult the priest.

The end of the scene

Agamemnon leaves the stage to go in search of Calchas.

- What are your initial impressions of the character of Clytaemnestra?
- What is your impression of the relationship between Clytaemnestra and Agamemnon?
- What is the tone of Agamemnon's exit line? Do you feel any pity for him? Why?

CLYTAEMNESTRA They have my blessing. When is the wedding day? 690

AGAMEMNON When the moon is full.

CLYTAEMNESTRA Have you made the preliminary sacrifice to the goddess?

AGAMEMNON I am about to. We are ready for it.

CLYTAEMNESTRA And will you give the wedding feast afterwards?

AGAMEMNON First the sacrifice which I owe the gods. 695

CLYTAEMNESTRA Where shall we have the feast for the women?

AGAMEMNON Here, by the Argive ships . . .

CLYTAEMNESTRA I suppose we must. Let's hope it's all right.

AGAMEMNON You know what to do, my wife? Do as I say.

CLYTAEMNESTRA What do you mean? I'm used to obeying you. 700

AGAMEMNON The bridegroom and I . . .

CLYTAEMNESTRA Will do what? Without me? I have my role.

AGAMEMNON Will give away our daughter, with the Greeks.

CLYTAEMNESTRA And what about me, while that happens?

AGAMEMNON Go back to Argos and look after the girls. 705

CLYTAEMNESTRA Abandoning my daughter? Who will hold the torch?

AGAMEMNON I'll light the wedding flame.

CLYTAEMNESTRA That's not the way it's done. This is no trivial matter.

AGAMEMNON It's not right for you to mingle with the crowd of soldiers.

CLYTAEMNESTRA It is right for a mother to give away her child in
marriage. 710

AGAMEMNON But it's not right to leave your daughters alone at home.

CLYTAEMNESTRA They are perfectly safe in their quarters.

AGAMEMNON Do as I say.

CLYTAEMNESTRA No, by the goddess queen of Argos,
You can go off and do what you must; 715
I'll go inside and see to those things
That girls must be permitted on their wedding day.

AGAMEMNON Oh dear, that plan came to nothing. My hope
Of sending my wife out of the way has failed.
I try to be clever, play tricks upon my loved ones, 720
But I am totally defeated.
But still together with the soothsayer Calchas
I shall find out what the goddess wills,
Even if it's hard for me, this turmoil for Greece.
A wise man should keep a good and honourable wife 725
At home – or no wife at all.

SECOND CHORAL ODE (SECOND *STASIMON*) (727–65)

In an abrupt change of tone, the Chorus launch into a dramatic, rhapsodic account of the cataclysm that awaits Troy. As on occasion in other tragedies, the Chorus here seem to step out of character and take on a prophetic role. They assert that the expedition will sail. They conjure up rich, visual images of the Greek armada, the savagery of the fighting and the fall of Troy (745–9), the reaction of the Trojan women to the fate which awaits them (751) and their attitude to Helen (760–5). Nothing is said of Iphigeneia, but the implication is that the sacrifice will take place.

727 Simois The river that flows just outside Troy.

730 Ilium Troy's citadel, also known as Pergamon (745). Troy was built by Poseidon and Apollo (731) for its founder Laomedon.

732 Cassandra A daughter of Priam and priestess of Apollo, who gave her the gift of prophecy; when she refused to sleep with him, Apollo punished her with the curse that nobody would believe her prophecies, thinking her to be mad. The ancient Greeks believed that madness resulted from inspiration by a deity, and treated the affected person with awe. Here Cassandra tosses her head in madness and wears a laurel wreath (733), the emblem of Apollo.

739 Ares The god of war is presented as travelling with the Greek army as they attack the Trojans defending their city (736–40). Ares comes with his bronze shield (739), a detail appropriate to a story from the Bronze Age.

742 Dioscuri The 'sons of Zeus' (see **'Leda's children'**, p. 6) were Castor and Pollux, brothers of Helen and Clytaemnestra. Turned after their death into stars, often associated with the constellation Gemini, they were thought to protect sailors, appearing in storms as St Elmo's fire. It is fitting to mention them as the Greek fleet sails to bring back Helen.

752–3 Helen . . . will be weak / With grief In the *Iliad* Helen is aware of her shameful position in Troy (see book 3), yet she receives sympathetic treatment from Priam and Hector. In the *Odyssey*, after the fall of Troy, she is back in Sparta living with Menelaus.

756 As they stand by their looms Weaving was a traditional activity for women in the ancient world. The Chorus picture the wives of the Trojans and their allies from nearby Lydia wondering whose property they will be when they are taken away to Greece as prisoners and slaves. A chorus of Greek women demonstrates empathy with the fate of the womenfolk of their enemies, the Trojans. Euripides in other plays too (*Trojan Women*, *Hecuba*) highlights the universal suffering of women in war.

CHORUS It will come to Simois
And its silvery swirling waters,
The host of the Greek army
Moving with ships and armour to Ilium, 730
The city of Troy, sacred to Apollo,
Where, I hear, Cassandra, wearing a fresh-leaved
Laurel crown, flings around her golden hair,
When the prophetic breath of the god
Constrains her. 735

On the battle towers
And round the walls of Troy
The Trojans will stand
As over the sea Ares with his bronze shield
Approaches in a convoy of handsome prowed ships 740
The streams of Simois, intent on taking from Priam
Helen, sister of the heavenly Dioscuri,
Back to the land of Greece by force of Greeks
Battling with shield and sword.

Surrounding Pergamon, Troy's citadel, 745
And the battle towers of stone,
He will pile heads torn from men's throats
In murderous fighting,
And ravage the city utterly,
Leaving the wife of Priam and his daughters 750
Weak with tears.
Helen, daughter of Zeus, will be weak
With grief for leaving her husband.
May neither I nor my children's children ever
Suffer like the rich Lydians and the Phrygians' wives 755
As they stand by their looms and say
To one another: 'Who will drag me by the hair,
Drawing from me tears, and pluck me like a flower
From my ruined home?'

Helen's guilt

Paris was often blamed for Helen's seduction and so for the Trojan War (446), but Agamemnon implied that Helen was equally culpable (75n) and here the Chorus condemn her (760, also 1210–11). The topic of responsibility for the war was a subject for fanciful debate, such as the Sophists (see **'Sophistry'**, p. 60) enjoyed: Gorgias, a prominent teacher of Euripides' day, wrote a provocative speech in praise of Helen; and Euripides himself wrote a play (*Helen*) in which Helen never went to Troy, but was spirited away to Egypt and the war was fought over a phantom (see **'Supernatural intervention'**, p. 102).

763 the Muses Goddesses of inspiration. The Greeks believed that an artist's talent for creating poetry, music or art was breathed into him by one of the Muses. Here Euripides, as often, casts doubt on the truth of a myth, the traditional account of Helen's birth. He himself, of course, 'rewrote' myths, including the story of Helen (see **'Helen's guilt'**, above).

● What is the function of this choral ode here in the drama of the play?
○ How could the staging of the ode highlight its significance?

THIRD EPISODE (766–994)

Clytaemnestra and Agamemnon have left the stage. Achilles, looking for Agamemnon, enters the stage and addresses the Chorus.

Achilles' character

A member of the play's original audience would have had a picture of Achilles from the *Iliad*, in which his anger and stubbornness, provoked by a bitter argument with Agamemnon over a slave girl, drive the action of the poem. The Greek audience would have found interesting comparisons between Achilles in the *Iliad* and the youthful, inexperienced character of this play, before he went to Troy, with little to rely on but his semi-divine ancestry.

773–4 This lust for war . . . Is the gods' doing The army is impatient to fight. Thucydides the historian, Euripides' contemporary, comments on the excitement that gripped the young men of Greece at the beginning of the Peloponnesian War; he also uses similar language to that of Euripides here (773) for the mood of the Greeks, to describe the irrational passion which induced the Athenian assembly to vote for the disastrous expedition against Sicily in 415 BC (see **'Leadership 2'**, p. 28). Even after the defeat in Sicily, there was a pro-war party in Athens, fanning war hysteria. As elsewhere, Euripides seems to be investing the characters and the action of the play with aspects of his own contemporary world. For the idea that passion is the work of the gods, see 70n, 1222.

It's your fault, offspring of the long-necked swan,   760
    If the saying is true that Leda bore you
    To a winged bird, Zeus in altered shape,
    Or stories in the writings of the Muses
      Have suggested this to men
      Out of season and wrongly.   765

ACHILLES Where is the commander of the Greeks?
  Will someone please tell him that Achilles,
  The son of Peleus, is at the gates, looking for him?
  Waiting here at the Euripus is not the same
  For all of us. Some are unmarried and sit here   770
  On the shore, having left empty homes;
  Others have wives and children.
  This lust for war that has struck Greece
  Is the gods' doing. I speak only for myself.
  Others who wish will speak on their own behalf.   775

776 Pharsalus In Thessaly, also known as Phthia.

785 Queen Modesty Achilles, expecting to see Agamemnon or a servant, is astonished by the appearance from the tent of a noblewoman. He has no idea who she is, and greets her with chivalrous courtesy.

788 I'm pleased that you respect modesty Achilles goes on to confirm the good impression he makes on Clytaemnestra. His strong sense of decorum (793–4, 797–8), part of a noble's code of honour, would make him an ideal son-in-law in her eyes (see **'Honour and reputation'**, p. 28).

Clytaemnestra and Achilles

There is a touch of Greek New Comedy (see **'Domestic drama'**, p. 46) about this exchange between Clytaemnestra and Achilles. Here we have two grand people, a queen and a hero, talking about mundane matters of etiquette. This strips them of their glamour, and makes them seem very ordinary. Clytaemnestra is keen to see the man who is to be her future son-in-law, and is pleased by his conduct (788n) and the thought of his divine birth, which she mentions frequently (784, 800, 865, 867). He has no idea of the supposed betrothal, and this misunderstanding is exploited by Euripides to comic effect. Both realise that they have been tricked (810); Clytaemnestra feels shame (813) which Achilles tries to allay (815), and they both feel humiliated (818), not knowing why the marriage has been proposed.

I have left Pharsalus and my father Peleus
To wait here at the narrow waters of Euripus,
Keeping my Myrmidons in check. They press
Me, saying, 'Achilles, why do we delay? How much
Longer must we wait before we sail for Troy?   780
Do something, if you're going to! Or lead the army home,
Don't wait on the dithering of the sons of Atreus.'

CLYTAEMNESTRA I heard your words from inside,
Son of the sea-goddess, and so I have come out.

ACHILLES Queen Modesty, who can this lady be,   785
That I see, so handsome?

CLYTAEMNESTRA I'm not surprised you don't know me: we've never met.
I'm pleased that you respect modesty.

ACHILLES Who are you? Why are you out in this crowd of Greeks,
A woman among men armed with shields?   790

CLYTAEMNESTRA I am Leda's daughter, Clytaemnestra, and
My husband is Lord Agamemnon.

ACHILLES Admirably brief! But to me it is
Not honourable to talk to women.

CLYTAEMNESTRA Stop! Don't run away! Give me your hand   795
To pledge a happy marriage.

ACHILLES What? Take your hand? I'd feel shame
Before Agamemnon to touch what I should not.

CLYTAEMNESTRA Of course you may! You're going to marry
My daughter, son of the divine sea-nymph!   800

ACHILLES Marry! I'm speechless, lady.
Are you mad? You're making this up!

CLYTAEMNESTRA It's natural to feel shy, meeting in-laws
For the first time, to discuss the wedding.

ACHILLES I've never sought your daughter's hand, lady,   805
Nor have the sons of Atreus talked of marriage to me.

CLYTAEMNESTRA How can this be? You are puzzled
By what I say. And your words amaze me.

ACHILLES And well they may. We can both assume
We've both been equally deceived.   810

CLYTAEMNESTRA I have been monstrously abused. I've come
In search of a non-existent marriage, it seems.
I am embarrassed.

Twists in the plot

As Achilles makes to leave the stage, the Old Man calls to him and Clytaemnestra from the tent (819–20). His intervention provides the second unexpected entry of the scene (the first being that of Clytaemnestra), and the second surprise for Achilles in his search for Agamemnon. The Old Man's reluctance to appear (826) allows for some visual and verbal comedy as he peers from the tent.

Names

The characters of this play are often addressed by the names of their parents (see 196n). Achilles is called son of Peleus / of Thetis, of a goddess / sea-nymph; Clytaemnestra is 'Leda's daughter'. Here, quaintly, the Old Man addresses Achilles by reference to his grandfather, who was of the old servant's own generation (819). See also 'Ancestry', p. 68.

835 Loyal first to you, and to your husband less The reason why the Old Man stresses his primary loyalty to Clytaemnestra will become apparent (837ff).

842 What spirit [*alastōr*] has possessed him? An *alastōr* was a supernatural spirit or Fury. The Furies hounded those who had committed a crime, especially murder, until retribution had been fully sought and recompense paid. Clytaemnestra's question implies that only the need for vengeance could explain her husband's wanting to kill his daughter: he must be possessed by some such spirit.

844 But where? It is unclear whether this is unintentionally comic or whether Clytaemnestra is so distraught by the news that she can't think properly. Surely she knows that the expedition is intending to sail to Troy!

845 home of Dardanus Dardanus was an early settler in Troy, where he received land from its first king, Teucer.

Quick-pace dialogue

Euripides' use of two-line dialogue in the exchange between Clytaemnestra and Achilles skilfully allows him the opportunity to say more, whilst maintaining the effect of *stichomythia*. He switches to *stichomythia* upon the entry of the Old Man. Clytaemnestra's shock is revealed in her long list of questions. Her initial disbelief (838) gradually turns into the grim realisation that her daughter is to be sacrificed (846).

ACHILLES Someone has made a mockery of us both.
But try to disregard it. Make light of it!   815

CLYTAEMNESTRA Goodbye! I can't look you in the eye any more.
I've been put in a false position and humiliated.

ACHILLES I feel the same. I'm going to find your husband inside.

OLD MAN Stranger, grandson of Aeacus, wait. You, son of a goddess,
And you, Leda's daughter!   820

ACHILLES Who's that calling, peeping like some timid creature
through the door?

OLD MAN A slave. I can't make pretences. That's my lot.

ACHILLES Whose slave? Not mine. Mine aren't with Agamemnon's.

OLD MAN I belong to the lady with you outside, passed on by her
father Tyndareus.

ACHILLES We're waiting. Explain, please, why you stopped me.   825

OLD MAN Are you two alone out there?

ACHILLES Just the two of us. Come out of the royal tent.

OLD MAN Fate and what good sense I have, preserve my dear ones.

ACHILLES He'll take forever. He's frightened.

CLYTAEMNESTRA Don't waste time on shaking hands, if you've
something to say.   830

OLD MAN You know me, don't you, loyal to you and to your children?

CLYTAEMNESTRA I do, old servant of my home.

OLD MAN And Lord Agamemnon received me as part of your dowry.

CLYTAEMNESTRA You came with me to Argos. You've always been mine.

OLD MAN That's right. Loyal first to you, and to your husband less.   835

CLYTAEMNESTRA Now tell us what you're hiding.

OLD MAN Your daughter . . . Her father plans to kill her, with his own hand.

CLYTAEMNESTRA What? Take back your words, Old Man. You're mad!

OLD MAN With a sword, murdering her pale neck, poor girl.

CLYTAEMNESTRA Oh! . . . Is my husband out of his mind?   840

OLD MAN He's sane, except in his attitude to you and your child.

CLYTAEMNESTRA For what reason? What spirit has possessed him?

OLD MAN Some prophecy, Calchas says – so that the fleet can sail.

CLYTAEMNESTRA But where? How I suffer! My daughter, killed by
her own father!

OLD MAN To the home of Dardanus, so that Menelaus can get back Helen. 845

CLYTAEMNESTRA Then Iphigeneia must die, to bring Helen home?

The Old Man

The Old Man, a slave, showed himself in the Prologue to have greater wisdom and a clearer sense of morality than Agamemnon (45n). In this episode he has ensured that Clytaemnestra is no longer deceived.

● What does the Old Man contribute to the theme of freedom and slavery in the play? What else does he bring to the play?

Supplication 1

When someone making a supplication or entreaty (864) touches the other person's knee or right hand or chin (873–5), he puts himself under the protection of Zeus. The person to whom the appeal is made is thus put under pressure to grant the request, for to reject a suppliant incurred Zeus' anger. The custom was based on the principle that the strong should show respect and compassion to the weak.

864 I am not ashamed to kneel before you Clytaemnestra kneeling to Achilles presents a striking picture, but there is something anomalous in the situation. She is a queen, a mature woman; he is a young man (899), with – as yet – no great status. She is also enlisting his support against her husband (see **'Friends and enemies 3'**, p. 62) and his commanding officer. But she is so desperate for Achilles' help that she puts aside her pride. What seems to matter is that he is the son of a goddess, while she is a mere mortal (865, 867).

Sophistry

Euripides was much influenced by the contemporary intellectual life of Athens, where teachers known as Sophists encouraged scepticism, debate and enquiry. Sophistic arguments often centred on the clever use of persuasive rhetoric, and though an argument may have been technically weak, when presented well it could appear to be the stronger (see 311n). Here Clytaemnestra says that Achilles ought to defend Iphigeneia because she had been betrothed to him, even if he didn't know it (868). Achilles was called Iphigeneia's husband (872), and so he should defend her now.

869 crowned with flowers A crown was an important part of the bride's dress, but it would also be worn by a sacrificial animal (see **'Greek marriage customs'**, p. 32, and **'Sacrifice'**, p. 46). Flowers link the themes of marriage and sacrifice in the play (1039).

OLD MAN Exactly. Her father will sacrifice your child to Artemis.

CLYTAEMNESTRA What about the marriage, with which he lured
    me from home?

OLD MAN It was to get you to bring her cheerfully to marry her to Achilles.

CLYTAEMNESTRA Daughter, you have come to your death – as has
    your mother too.   850

OLD MAN Both of you suffer grievously. Agamemnon has done
    something terrible.

CLYTAEMNESTRA I'm going. I can't contain my welling tears.

OLD MAN It's terrible to lose a child. Don't stop your tears.

CLYTAEMNESTRA But, Old Man, how do you know this? How did
    you find out?

OLD MAN I was on my way with a letter, about the one he'd sent
    before.   855

CLYTAEMNESTRA Telling me not to bring the child to her death, or
    confirming it?

OLD MAN Not to bring her. Your husband saw sense at that time.

CLYTAEMNESTRA Then why don't you give me the letter you have?

OLD MAN Menelaus took it from me. He caused this disaster.

CLYTAEMNESTRA Child of Thetis, son of Peleus, do you hear this?   860

ACHILLES I heard your grief. For me too this is no light matter.

CLYTAEMNESTRA They're going to kill my child, deceiving her by
    talk of marrying you.

ACHILLES I too hold your husband to blame. I find this difficult.

CLYTAEMNESTRA I am not ashamed to kneel before you.

    I am a mortal, you the son of a goddess. Why should I be proud?   865
    Could anything be more important than a child?
    Stand by me, goddess' son, in my ill fortune
    And by the girl it's wrong to call your wife, but still she's yours.
    I brought her, crowned with flowers, to marry you,
    But now I lead her to her slaughter. You will be reproached,   870
    If you don't defend her. Even if you were not joined
    In marriage, you were called the poor girl's husband.
    By your beard, your hand, and by your knee I beseech you
    And by your mother's name – you must defend your own name,
    Which has destroyed me.   875

Friends and enemies 3

Clytaemnestra presents herself as deserted by her husband, with no friends to defend her (876). The bond between friends and kin (*philoi*) was the strongest in Greek society, in which 'Help your friends and harm your enemies' was an almost unquestioned principle. Agamemnon has betrayed his family and so Clytaemnestra must overcome any compunction she feels at thwarting her husband. See 864n, **'Friends and enemies 1'**, p. 24.

876 altar of refuge A god's altar provides sanctuary to suppliants. Clytaemnestra is relying on Achilles' semi-divine ancestry (865, 867, 874).

Motherhood

Clytaemnestra uses her position as a mother to try to win Achilles over to help her prevent the sacrifice (866). She even begs him to consider his own mother (874) and the dishonour done to her indirectly via him. The Old Man comments on the particular horror of losing a child (853), and the Chorus understand the wrong she feels (883–4).

Achilles' self-assessment

Achilles begins his reply by talking about himself. He acknowledges that he is young (899) and claims to be aware of the danger of extreme emotions (885–90). In the *Iliad* he is a byword for excess, and here ironically he gives us a glimpse of the man he is to be. It is Achilles' passion and independent spirit (895) that will isolate him from his fellow Greeks in the *Iliad*, and he will disobey the sons of Atreus when he finds their leadership wanting (893–4).

891 Cheiron See 679n.

896 I'll honour Ares He means that he will not be a coward in battle.

Achilles and Clytaemnestra (National Theatre, London, 2004).

I have no other altar of refuge, no friend at my side.
You hear Agamemnon's cruel effrontery.
I have come here, as you see, a woman among sailors;
They have their value, but they are
Undisciplined, prepared for any crime. 880
If you have the courage to raise your hand in my defence,
We are saved. If not, there is no salvation for us.

CHORUS It is a wondrous thing to be a mother; it generates
Deep love. We all do our best for our children.

ACHILLES My pride can carry me away. But I have learnt 885
To grieve at setbacks, and take delight
When things go well, in moderation.
Such men can reckon to live good and sensible lives.
There are times when it is pleasant not to think too deeply
And others when we need to use our judgement. 890
I was brought up by Cheiron, a man of deep piety,
Who taught me simple ways.
I shall obey the sons of Atreus if their leadership is sound,
But not when it's misguided.
Here and in Troy I'll be an independent spirit 895
And in fighting, as far as I can, I'll honour Ares.
You have suffered cruelly at the hands of your dearest.
I feel such compassion for you that I'll do
All a young man can to reduce your suffering.
Never will your daughter, my promised bride, 900
Be slaughtered by her father. I won't allow
Your husband to use me to weave his web of lies.
Otherwise it will be my name, even if I do not touch the sword,
Which will kill your child. The responsibility will be
Your husband's, but *my* body will be defiled if she dies 905
Because of me and her marrying me.
The girl has suffered intolerable wrong,
Treated with amazing disrespect.

911 I am not Peleus' son, but some avenging Fury's Achilles means that he is his own self, sane and responsible: he would be mad, possessed (842n), to allow his name to be implicated in Iphigeneia's death.

916 Mount Sipylos, the barbarians' stronghold Mount Sipylos was in Lydia, Asia Minor, and associated with Troy; see also 354n and **'Barbarians and Troy'**, p. 8.

919–20 barley grains . . . holy water Achilles implies disparagingly that the paraphernalia of sacrifice (see **'Sacrifice'**, p. 46) will be somehow contaminated in Calchas' hands.

Calchas

Agamemnon and Menelaus have already expressed cynical views of priests (495n), including Calchas. In the *Iliad* and in Aeschylus' *Agamemnon* Calchas is a respected priest. It is Calchas in *Iliad* 1 who interprets the plague sent by Apollo on the Greek army, which results in Agamemnon demanding Achilles' slave girl from Achilles. Achilles here (919–22) anticipates the antipathy he will feel towards him at Troy.

Achilles' name and reputation 1

Reputation is very important to Homeric heroes; for Achilles, in the *Iliad* and here, it is tantamount to his honour. (1) He agrees to defend Iphigeneia because he feels that if she dies he will be reproached because she will be thought to be his wife (872, 906). As he will be implicated in her death (904–5), his name will suffer disrepute. (2) Agamemnon, with fateful misjudgement, used Achilles' name to deceive his wife (126); the Old Man knew better (131–4). Achilles is now angry, not so much because an innocent young girl may be slaughtered, but because his name has been used without his permission (925–7). He is insulted, his honour has been slighted by Agamemnon (924); he would have agreed to the marriage with Iphigeneia for the greater good of the Greeks and their expedition to Troy, but now he has been dishonoured he will defend himself and Iphigeneia. See **'Honour and reputation'**, p. 28.

935 I seem to you a mighty god Achilles' words seem hubristic, but the Chorus do not seem to think so in their response. Achilles perhaps refers to Clytaemnestra's associating him with an altar of refuge (876n).

Achilles' speech

- What is your impression of Achilles? Is he practising the moderation and control which he professes?
- Do you find his sense of honour noble or egotistic?
- How would you describe the tone of his speech?

I am the basest of the Greeks – rather I am nothing,
And Menelaus is more a man in comparison –   910
I am not Peleus' son, but some avenging Fury's, if my name
Is held responsible for murder on your husband's behalf.
By Nereus, reared in the waves, father of Thetis, who bore me,
Lord Agamemnon will not touch your daughter;
He will not lay a finger even to harm her dress –   915
Or else Mount Sipylos, the barbarians' stronghold,
Will win renown as home to the warrior race,
While Phthia will be nowhere mentioned.
Calchas the prophet will bring his miserable barley grains
And holy water, but what sort of prophet is a man   920
Who, when he's right, for every grain
Of truth speaks much that's false, and when he's wrong he disappears.
I say this not because of the marriage – countless girls
Would bed me – but because Agamemnon has insulted me.
He should have *asked* to use my name, to snare   925
Your daughter. That's what persuaded Clytaemnestra
To hand over her daughter to her husband.
I would have done it for the Greeks, if our mission
To Troy depended on it. I would not have refused
To advance the cause of those with whom I served.   930
Now I am nothing, the other leaders do not care
Whether they treat me well or badly.
But my sword will know whose blood will stain it,
Before we go to Troy, should anyone take your daughter
From me. Stay calm. I seem to you a mighty god.   935
I am not, but I will be.
CHORUS Your words, son of Peleus, are worthy of you
        And of the sea-spirit, the august goddess.

939 Oh, how can I thank you without excess Clytaemnestra is delighted by Achilles' offer of help. Her reaction to the good news shows she sees that he respects decorum and etiquette, and is keen to show moderation.

944–5 there is merit . . . Helping those in trouble There was a fundamental principle in Greek society, reflected in the ritual of supplication (see **'Supplication 1'**, p. 60), that the strong should show respect and compassion to the weak, who were under the protection of Zeus (see also 968). Clytaemnestra is as concerned as Achilles with appearances.

947 But should you marry her Clytaemnestra cannot shake off the hope that Achilles may marry her daughter.

Supplication 2
Although Iphigeneia is unmarried and Clytaemnestra knows that it is inappropriate for her daughter to supplicate him (953), she seems to feel that Achilles may be flattered by this prospect. Her maternal instinct is to protect her daughter and her honour (956), but if Achilles' self-esteem requires it, then Clytaemnestra is willing to allow her daughter to come out.

Achilles' name and reputation 2
It is again Achilles' concern for his reputation that makes him decline Clytaemnestra's offer (958–61).

965 I will not lie Achilles' pledge is designed to set him firmly apart from Agamemnon.

Achilles' oath
Achilles swears on his life to protect Iphigeneia (966–7). As the traditional story is that he will live and sail to Troy, the audience may infer that perhaps Iphigeneia will be saved after all.

972 He's too scared of the army This was Menelaus' opinion too (492).

CLYTAEMNESTRA Oh, how can I thank you without excess

    Or say too little and undo my thanks? 940

    Good people hate to hear themselves acclaimed,

    When it's too highly. I am ashamed to be so pitiful,

    For suffering which is mine and should not touch you.

    Yet there is merit in a good man, even if he's not involved,

    Helping those in trouble. Pity us. Our suffering 945

    Is pitiful. I thought that you would be my son-in-law,

    But found my hope was empty. But should you marry her,

    My daughter's death would bring bad luck for you.

    You must do all you can to avoid that.

    From start to finish what you said was right. 950

    With your good will, my daughter will be saved.

    Do you want her to supplicate you, at your knee?

    It's not right for an unmarried girl to do so, but if you wish

    She will come out, her modesty intact.

    But if we can achieve the same without her presence 955

    Let her stay inside: so dignity is preserved.

    But we must at all cost plead for you to help.

ACHILLES Don't bring your child to see me. Let's not risk

    The censure of ignorant people, lady.

    The army gathered here, free from daily chores, 960

    Loves spiteful gossip and foul-mouthed abuse.

    Whether you entreat me or not, you'll find me

    The same; I have but one overriding aim:

    To end your suffering.

    Of one thing you can be sure: I will not lie. 965

    May I die if I fall to lying and abuse,

    But not die, if I save the girl.

CLYTAEMNESTRA Eternal blessings on you for helping those in trouble.

ACHILLES Then listen, how we may succeed.

CLYTAEMNESTRA What? I can only listen to you. 970

ACHILLES Let's try to persuade her father to think again.

CLYTAEMNESTRA He's weak. He's too scared of the army.

Persuasion

Achilles wants to settle the dispute by reason and not by force (971), believing that the army would accept that. He wants to avoid jeopardising his relationship with Agamemnon (978, how different from the *Iliad*!). See **'Achilles' character'**, p. 54. He urges Clytaemnestra to supplicate Agamemnon, as she has proved to him how effective her persuasive skills are. For Euripides' audience, persuasion was a double-edged skill. In his day at Athens, where great matters of state were decided in the citizens' assembly by a vote, power fell into the hands of those with the greatest rhetorical ability and a new breed of politician emerged, the demagogue. The dominant assembly speakers manipulated the volatile public and, with the Sophists, were held by many to be responsible for the moral decline of Athens. See 311n.

- How realistic is Achilles' view of the army here (979), given what he has already said?

984 But if we don't achieve my wish Clytaemnestra is thinking ahead, preparing for every eventuality to ensure that she saves her daughter.

Ancestry

In the world of epic, men and women are measured against the reputation of their predecessors. Achilles urges Clytaemnestra not to bring shame on her family (989–91, see 480). The consciousness of family ties makes it normal to swear by one's ancestors (913) or call on them in prayer (1191). This custom was so prevalent that when Menelaus (452) and Iphigeneia (1191) invoke their infamous ancestors, the irony seems unconscious.

993 If the gods are wise Characters in Euripides' plays reflect the range of opinion in his day about religion. Some have an overall belief in the power of the gods to influence events, especially to send misfortune, and in divine justice. Others express the scepticism of the age, ridiculing the tales about the gods and questioning or denying their existence. But Clytaemnestra's words need not suggest profound disillusion.

The end of the episode

- How attractive a character do you find Achilles?
- Does Clytaemnestra appear to be vulnerable or manipulative?

ACHILLES Argument can conquer fear.

CLYTAEMNESTRA Small hope. But tell me what to do.

ACHILLES First plead with him not to kill the child.   975
    If he resists, come to me. But if he agrees,
    I need do nothing. That solves the problem.
    My relations with him, who is my friend, will improve
    And the army would not find fault with me,
    If I settled the matter by reason, not by force.   980
    If that's achieved to your satisfaction and
    Your family's, I need not be involved.

CLYTAEMNESTRA How sensible! We must do what you say.
    But if we don't achieve my wish,
    Where will I find you? Where must I go,   985
    Poor woman, to find your helping hand?

ACHILLES I will be there to protect you, when you need it.
    Don't let anyone see you passing agitated
    Through the crowd of Greeks. Don't put to shame
    Your family home. Tyndareus does not deserve   990
    A slur on his name, which is great among the Greeks.

CLYTAEMNESTRA I agree. Lead on. I must be your slave. You are a
       just man.
    If the gods are wise, you will be rewarded.
    If not, why should we trouble to do anything?

THIRD CHORAL ODE (THIRD *STASIMON*) (995–1055)

Achilles and Clytaemnestra have left the stage. The Chorus, as if to forget the present, recall the joyous wedding feast of Achilles' parents, Peleus and Thetis, of which Agamemnon talked to Clytaemnestra (675–81). They evoke a picture of a golden age, not long gone, when gods mixed with mortals. It accords with their star-struck view of the Greek warriors in the *Parodos*, but it is not just a nostalgic reminiscence. They recall the glorious marriage of Achilles' parents to contrast it with the marriage which is not to be, with the terrible reality of Iphigeneia's sacrifice, and they end in a despairing lament for the depths to which mankind has sunk.

The wedding feast of Peleus and Thetis

We are presented with an idyllic image of the wedding feast of Peleus and Thetis, depicting dancing, music and drinking. The Centaurs are present, but there is none of the barbaric behaviour which they showed at the wedding of Pirithous and Hippodameia amongst the Lapiths, where they tried to abduct the bride. There is no discordant note in this account, no reference to the goddess Eris, whose wedding gift of the golden apple contributed to the start of the Trojan War (see *Background to the story*, p. v).

996 The god of marriage Hymenaeus or Hymen. His name is also given to the refrain of Greek wedding songs.

997 Libyan flute and lyre Greek choruses were accompanied by flute and pipes and the chorus members would have danced whilst they sang. Possibly the staging of this ode would have represented the wedding celebration.

999 Mount Pelion See 679n.

1001 fair-haired Muses See 763n. It is appropriate for these goddesses, like the god of marriage, to attend a divine wedding feast.

1008 son of Aeacus Peleus (see 673n).

1013 The Phrygian Ganymede Ganymede was the son of Laomedon and a descendant of Dardanus (845n). King Priam was his brother. He was abducted by Zeus or his eagle to be Zeus' cup-bearer because of his exceptional beauty. Zeus gave his father a pair of divine horses.

1021 Bacchus' bowl Bacchus, or Dionysus, was the god of wine, theatre and fertility. See *Introduction to the Greek Theatre*, pp. 112–15.

What a joyous sound   995
                  The god of marriage raised
         With Libyan flute and lyre that loves the dance
                        And pipes of reed,
                      When on Mount Pelion
                    Amid the feasting gods   1000
                     The fair-haired Muses
                   Came to Peleus' wedding,
                       Beating the ground
                   With their gold-sandalled feet;
                 And through the woods of Pelion   1005
            In the mountains where the Centaurs live
              They celebrated in melodious sounds
                  Thetis and the son of Aeacus.
                 And Dardanus' descendant,
                    Zeus' darling in his bed,   1010
                     Poured drink from bowls
                       With golden spouts,
                     The Phrygian Ganymede.
               And along the white-gleaming shore
                  The fifty daughters of Nereus   1015
                      Spinning in circles
                   Danced the wedding dance.

                 With crowns and foliage of fir
               A mounted troop of Centaurs came
                    To the banquet of the gods   1020
                      And Bacchus' bowl.

1022 Nereus' daughter Thetis was one of Nereus' 50 daughters (675, 1015, see 226n).

1024 Apollo's priestess-muse Apollo's priestess, the Pythia, at Delphi spoke the god's words in the form of oracles.

The prophecy foretelling Achilles' greatness
Euripides does not mention the part of the prophecy which said that Thetis' son would be greater than his father, the reason for Thetis' marriage to a human rather than another god; instead he focuses upon the son's future greatness. Achilles is presented as a 'great light' for Thessaly (1026), suggesting his essential contribution to the destruction of the 'famed land of Priam' (1028).

Achilles' armour
In *Iliad* 16 Achilles, who after his quarrel with Agamemnon refuses to fight, lends his armour to his dear friend Patroclus so that he may drive back the Trojans from the Greek ships. Patroclus loses his life to Hector, who strips the corpse of its armour. In *Iliad* 18 Achilles, maddened by grief and rage, presents himself unarmed to the Trojans as a result, and his mother (1031) offers him protection in the form of divinely wrought armour, made by Hephaestus (1030). The shield is famously described in detail by Homer in *Iliad* 18.

The sacrifice of Iphigeneia
Abruptly the Chorus break away from the joyful picture of the past to Iphigeneia's impending sacrifice. The detailed imagery, likening her to a sacrificial calf (1040), highlights the helplessness of the girl and the shocking intention to sacrifice her. The calf is young like Iphigeneia and unblemished, just as Iphigeneia's virgin status makes her pure. See **'Sacrifice'**, p. 46. The pathos and horror of the situation are emphasised further by the Chorus' direct address to Iphigeneia (1038ff).

1039 Will crown your glorious, flowing locks Again (see 869n) the crown links the context of marriage (1018) to that of sacrifice, in which animals were led to the altar wearing a crown or garland. Unmarried Greek girls wore their hair loose.

1047 the sons of Inachus The men of Argos, Agamemnon's kingdom, of which Inachus was the legendary first king.

And loud they cried 'Nereus' daughter,
The prophet Cheiron who knows
Apollo's priestess-muse has pronounced
That you will bear a child,   1025
A great light for Thessaly,
Who with the speared warriors of the Myrmidons
Will burn to ashes the famed land of Priam,
Wearing armour and helmet of gold,
Forged by Hephaestus,   1030
A gift from his godly mother Thetis
Who bore him.'
Blessed was the marriage
That the gods arranged
And the wedding song   1035
For the first of Nereus' noble daughters
And Peleus.

But on your head, Iphigeneia, the Argives
Will crown your glorious, flowing locks,
Like a dappled calf that comes unblemished   1040
From rocky mountain caves,
And stain with your own blood
Your human throat.
You were not brought up to hear
The pipe and whistles of the herdsmen,   1045
But at your mother's side to be
Among the sons of Inachus
A bride dressed for her wedding.

Moral decline

The Chorus are horrified that an innocent girl is about to be sacrificed. Their lament for the decline in moral standards would have a resonance for an Athenian audience. Thucydides charted the corrupting effects on the Athenians of their long war against Sparta, and the appalling atrocities committed in the name of Athens (see **'The army'**, p. 36). The Sophists were blamed for undermining traditional values, but the whole tenor of public debate had been debased and the voters in the assembly were regularly led by opportunistic considerations of self-interest rather than principle. See **'Persuasion'**, p. 68.

● What is the dramatic impact of this choral song at this point in the play?

FOURTH EPISODE (1056–1236)

Clytaemnestra, in pursuit of her husband, addresses the Chorus. When Agamemnon enters, it is clear (1064–6) that he does not know that his wife is aware of his plan. Once again Euripides employs dramatic irony.

1062 His wicked scheme against his children Clytaemnestra may feel there is a threat to the whole family (see 1151–2), but there is some exaggeration here.

1068 Send her out to be with her father Agamemnon has just told Clytaemnestra that he has things to tell her that are not appropriate for Iphigeneia's ears. This change of plan is typical of the changeability he has displayed elsewhere in the play.

1071 before marriage Agamemnon keeps up his pretence of an animal sacrifice, talking of the paraphernalia of sacrifice (see **'Sacrifice'**, p. 46).

Clytaemnestra confronts Agamemnon (1082–1102)

Clytaemnestra has told her daughter offstage of Agamemnon's intentions (1075–6). She has agreed to Achilles' suggestion that she plead with Agamemnon to spare Iphigeneia (975). In the manner of a lawyer she begins to cross-question him (1087, see 1200n). In an Athenian law-court defendants were allowed to bring their weeping wife and children into the court to sway the jurors' decision. Clytaemnestra has decided to involve her own children (1075–7) to put emotional pressure on Agamemnon. He had dreaded this meeting with Iphigeneia and Orestes (441–5). Iphigeneia, in childlike fashion, covers her face with her robes (1081) and stands in silence as Clytaemnestra exposes his pretences (1087–1102).

● What aspects of Clytaemnestra's character do we see in this sharp exchange with her husband?

Where does the face of Decency or Virtue
  Have any power,   1050
When godlessness holds sway
And Virtue lies neglected,
  Lawlessness prevails
And men have no common will
  To avert the anger of the gods?   1055

CLYTAEMNESTRA I have come out to look for my husband.
  He left his tent some time ago.
  My poor daughter is in tears
  Pouring out a litany of grief,
  Having learnt of the death her father plans.   1060
  I heard mention that Agamemnon had passed nearby.
  His wicked scheme against his children
  Will soon be revealed.
AGAMEMNON Daughter of Leda, I'm glad to find you
  Out here. I want to say, away from the girl's hearing,   1065
  Things which a bride should not hear.
CLYTAEMNESTRA What is it?
AGAMEMNON Send her out to be with her father.
  The holy water is prepared and offerings
  Of barley, to throw into the purifying flame,   1070
  And calves which must be offered before marriage
  To the goddess Artemis, to spurt black blood.
CLYTAEMNESTRA You use fine words, but I don't know
  How I could find fine words for what you do.
  Daughter, come out. You know exactly what   1075
  Your father plans. And bring your brother Orestes
  With you. Wrap him in your robe.
  So here she is, obedient to you.
  But I shall speak for her and for myself.
AGAMEMNON Child, why do you weep? Not pleased to see me? 1080
  Why do you look down and cover your face?
CLYTAEMNESTRA (*sighs*) Where shall I begin on my misfortunes?
  Every one could be my first or last –
  Or altogether anywhere!

The murder of Tantalus

The bloody story of the murder of Clytaemnestra's first husband and child by Agamemnon (1109–17) is found only in this play, and perhaps is an invention of Euripides. No motive is given for the murder; and the only Tantalus known in traditional mythology is Agamemnon's grandfather (see **'House of Pelops'**, p. 36).

AGAMEMNON What is this? You all come at me, as one,   1085
You look confused, disturbed.

CLYTAEMNESTRA I have a question. Answer, husband, like an
honourable man.

AGAMEMNON No need to tell me what to do. Ask.

CLYTAEMNESTRA Your daughter and mine – do you intend to kill her?

AGAMEMNON What! That's outrageous! You have no right to have
such thoughts.   1090

CLYTAEMNESTRA Calm down! Answer my question.

AGAMEMNON If you ask a reasonable question, you'll get a
reasonable answer.

CLYTAEMNESTRA That is my question. Answer that, no other.

AGAMEMNON O sovereign destiny and fate and my controlling fortune!

CLYTAEMNESTRA And mine and hers, one destiny for three
ill-fated people.   1095

AGAMEMNON How have I wronged you?

CLYTAEMNESTRA You ask me that? You've lost your mind.

AGAMEMNON I am destroyed. My secret is betrayed.

CLYTAEMNESTRA I know everything, what you plan to do to me.
Your very silence and your sighs reveal   1100
That you admit it. Don't trouble yourself
To make a lengthy speech.

AGAMEMNON I'll not say anything. What is the sense
By telling lies of adding to my misfortune
Shamelessness?   1105

CLYTAEMNESTRA Then listen. I'll use plain words,
No more obscure riddles.
First – I'll get this reproach in first –
You married me against my will, took me by force,
Murdering my husband Tantalus.   1110
You tore my child violently from my breast
And dashed him to the ground.
My brothers, sons of Zeus, went after you
Galloping on horseback.
It was my father Tyndareus who rescued you   1115
When you appealed to him, and then you took me
To your bed. You will bear witness

1120–3 Modest and chaste . . . I was a rare catch Clytaemnestra promotes herself as the model of a good Greek wife, loyal to her husband (1120) and careful to protect her reputation, which would redound to his credit (1122). The Greek audience would have found this picture very different from that familiar from Aeschylus' *Agamemnon* (see **'Clytaemnestra 1'**, p. 42, and **'Clytaemnestra 2'**, below).

1124 I have borne you this boy and three girls Clytaemnestra has fulfilled her duty as a wife, bearing her husband children, including a male heir.

1128 So that Menelaus gets back Helen Clytaemnestra here echoes the Chorus (752–65): everything comes back to Helen. See **'Helen's guilt'**, p. 54.

Friends and enemies 4

In the Greek, the word *echthista* ('most hated') is juxtaposed with *philtatois* ('most dear', 1130) implying that Helen is an enemy to Agamemnon, who ought to be protecting his family. The financial metaphors used in this translation (1128–30) mirror the original Greek.

Clytaemnestra 2

Clytaemnestra first appeared as a gracious lady, a devoted mother concerned for her children's welfare, but increasingly we see her strength. She is not prepared to sacrifice her traditional role in the wedding; she fights desperately, going to extreme lengths, to save her daughter; now, angered by Agamemnon's continuing deceptions, she disinters a monstrous crime from his past, the murder of her first husband and child. So she deprives him of all moral authority. This is the only extant play that gives a sympathetic picture of the suffering which drove her to one of the great crimes of mythology, which is already taking shape in her mind (1140–51, 1418). Her reference to the way she welcomed her husband when he returned home from his travels (1121) contrasts with her welcome of him on his return from Troy (1141, 1146). While Agamemnon is at Troy, she takes as her lover Aegisthus, his cousin and enemy (see **'House of Pelops'**, p. 36), and plots Agamemnon's death; on his triumphal return she lures him into a bath and kills him with an axe (see Aeschylus' *Agamemnon*).

That I was reconciled to you and to your family
And have been a blameless wife,
Modest and chaste, a credit to your home. 1120
I made you happy to come home, made you
Feel blessed too when you went abroad.
I was a rare catch. There's no shortage of bad wives.
I have borne you this boy and three girls.
Now you will rob me ruthlessly of one. 1125
If someone asks you why you'll kill her,
Tell me, what will you say? Or must I answer for you?
So that Menelaus gets back Helen – a fine deal,
To give your child as payment for a whore,
Pay for something vile with what is dearest to you. 1130
If you go off to war, leaving me at home,
And are away for years, what do you think
Will be my feelings for you – whenever I see
Iphigeneia's empty chair, her quarters empty,
And I sit alone in tears, singing lamentations for her? 1135
'Your father has destroyed you, child – the man
Who gave you life, that very man,
Has murdered you, no other, not by another's hand,
Leaving the family to pay.'
Little excuse will I and my remaining daughters need 1140
To give to you the welcome home
Which you deserve. So I beg you, don't make me
Commit a sin – or sin yourself!
Ah. When you sacrifice your child, what will you pray,
What blessings will you ask for as you murder her? 1145
A grim homecoming, ignoble as your setting out?
And what should I pray for you that is good
And right? I would have to think the gods are stupid,
If I were to wish a murderer well.
When you come back to Argos, will you embrace 1150
Your children? You cannot! Which of them will ever
Look at you, for fear of being killed herself?
Have you thought this through? Or is only your staff of office
Important to you, and your command?

Rhetoric 2

- How skilful is Clytaemnestra's speech? What devices of rhetoric does she employ (see **'Rhetoric 1'**, p. 30)?

Iphigeneia's appeal to her father

Iphigeneia finally speaks. She addresses her father in an intimate, innocent way, appealing frankly to emotion and sentiment. But her use of literary allusion (1170) and metaphor (1175) and the overall structure of her speech suggest a more sophisticated, mature mind.

1170 the voice of Orpheus Orpheus was a mythical musician, famous for his ability to sing and play. He was said to have charmed nature and even the gods themselves with his music.

1175 Here is my suppliant branch Branches of olive feature in the opening of Sophocles' *Oedipus Tyrannus*, where the people of Thebes come to ask for their king's help, but were not usual in a domestic setting. Iphigeneia supplicates her father by touching his knee (1176), and she offers her body, as a metaphorical branch of supplication, in a poignant appeal for mercy. For most, if not all, of her speech she is in a suppliant position (1186, 1205).

Agamemnon and Iphigeneia (National Theatre, London, 2004).

The right thing was for you to say to the Argives   1155
'Do you really want to sail to Phrygia?
If so, then vote whose child should die.'
That was the fair way, not that you should give
Your daughter as the chosen offering to the Greeks.
Menelaus should sacrifice Hermione, in front of her mother.   1160
This is his affair. Now I, who was faithful
To your bed, will lose a child, while she,
The tramp, will bring her little girl back home
To Sparta and live happily.
Answer me if any of what I say is wrong.   1165
If I'm right, I beg you, don't kill your child and mine!
Have some sense!

CHORUS Listen to her, Agamemnon. To save a child is right,
No one will argue against that.

IPHIGENEIA Father, if I had the voice of Orpheus,   1170
The power of persuasion by my songs, to make
The rocks follow me and charm anyone I wanted,
I would use it. But now I will use tears.
That makes sense – I can at least do that.
Here is my suppliant branch, my own body,   1175
Which my mother bore to you. I touch your knee.
Do not kill me before my time.
The light of day is sweet: don't drive me
Into the darkness of the underworld.
I was the first to call you father, the first   1180
Whom you called child. I was the first
To sit on your knees and give you sweet kisses
And have yours. You used to say, 'Shall I live,
My child, to see you happy in your husband's house,
Living and flourishing in a manner worthy of your father?'   1185
And I would clutch your beard, which now I hold again,
And say, 'And how will I see you? Shall I receive you
In my home, when you are old, and entertain you,
Nursing you in return for all your care of me?'

1191–2 by Pelops . . . by Atreus Invoking Pelops and Atreus seems ironic, as both these forefathers were infamous for their treatment of family, but see **'Ancestry'**, p. 68.

1200 Brother, you are too small to help Clytaemnestra had ordered Iphigeneia to bring her baby brother, Orestes (1076). Iphigeneia uses him now, almost as a prop, as the two supplicate their father (1204–5), in a scene reminiscent of an Athenian law-court (see **'Clytaemnestra confronts Agamemnon'**, p. 74). This is parodied in Aristophanes' *Wasps*, where the defendant on trial is a dog who has stolen some cheese from the kitchen. At an appropriate point in the proceedings, the dog's puppies are brought in to create sympathy.

The non-hero
Iphigeneia's attitude (1206–9) is characteristic of the ordinary, unheroic person. In contrast, the classic hero, Achilles in the *Iliad,* chose to die young, covered in glory, rather than have a long and inglorious life. Achilles was to regret this: he tells Odysseus, who visits him in the underworld, that he would rather be a slave in the world of the living than a king in the world of the dead (*Odyssey* 11).

1222 There is a raging passion in the army of the Greeks Again (see 773–4n) Agamemnon expresses the Greek army's frenzied longing for war in terms of sexual desire (the word for passion here is *Aphroditē*; see 70n). See *Background to the story*, p. v, for Aphrodite's role in the origins of the Trojan War.

Panhellenic mission
The original aim of the Greek expedition, to regain Helen and punish Paris, is now expanded. Expressed first by Menelaus as the need to assert Greek supremacy over the barbarians (353–4), it is now inflated in Agamemnon's rhetoric into a Panhellenic mission to 'stop the plunder of Greek wives' (1224, see also 1233) and preserve the freedom of Greece (1231).

I remember those conversations, but you forget 1190
And want to kill me. Don't, I pray, by Pelops
And by Atreus, your father, and by my mother here,
Who had pangs in bringing me to birth
And now is suffering a second agony.
What has Paris' match with Helen to do 1195
With me? How does it come to cause my death?
Look at me, look me in the eye and kiss me,
So that, if I don't persuade you, I can keep in death
At least this memory of you.
Brother, you are too small to help your dear ones 1200
But join in my tears, beseech your father to spare your sister.
However small, young children sense when things are wrong.
Look, father, he cannot speak, but he entreats you.
Respect me, pity me. Look! Your two dear ones
Entreat you by your beard – he is a baby, I'm grown up. 1205
All my arguments I can sum up in one and so prevail:
The light of day is what men most love,
The world below is nothing. Anyone who wants to die
Is mad. A miserable life is better than a noble death.
CHORUS Cursed Helen, you and your marriage have caused 1210
Great anguish to the sons of Atreus and their children.
AGAMEMNON I understand what's pitiable and what's not.
I love my children. I'd be mad not to.
It is dreadful for me to take this step,
And dreadful not to. This is what I *have* to do! 1215
You see the size of this army, the ring of ships
Around it, the number of Greek princes,
Leaders of bronze weaponry.
They will not have passage to the towers of Ilium,
Nor can they destroy the great seat of Troy, 1220
Unless I sacrifice you. So the prophet Calchas says.
There is a raging passion in the army of the Greeks
To sail as fast as possible to the barbarian land
And stop the plunder of Greek wives.

Agamemnon and Necessity 2

Agamemnon has not spoken since he said he would abandon deceit (1103–5). He clearly loves his children and is moved by his daughter's appeal. But he again claims that he is powerless (1215, 1230). He is the commander of the army, but he has no authority. He covers his weakness by insisting that his obligation to Greece outweighs that to his own family. See **'Agamemnon confounded'**, p. 34, and **'Agamemnon and Necessity 1'**, p. 38.

● Has Iphigeneia inherited her mother's rhetorical skills?
● Is Agamemnon motivated by a sense of duty or fear of the army? Does the scene with Iphigeneia make you believe more in his sincerity?

IPHIGENEIA'S FIRST SONG (MONODY) (1237–76)

A monody is a virtuosic aria, usually sung by a female character at a time of extreme emotion or passion. Euripides made increasing use of the device, reflecting possibly the growing musical skills of young actors. Its value is to heighten and intensify emotion, achieved by a variety of metres and a conspicuous repetition of words (1258, 1260, 1270) and perhaps complemented by expressive dance.

After Clytaemnestra has acknowledged defeat to both her daughter and the Chorus (1234–6), Iphigeneia breaks into song to convey her distress and isolation. She contrasts the fate of Paris, abandoned by his father Priam, but later saved, with her own, sacrificed by her father. As she reflects on the events that have brought her to imminent death, she focuses on the role of Helen (1260, 1274–6; see **'Helen's guilt'**, p. 54).

1240 Io, Io! With this invocation, Iphigeneia reproaches the glens of Ida for their part in Paris' upbringing. She considers herself dead (1239).

Paris

Before the birth of her son Paris, Hecuba dreamed that she was giving birth to a burning log. This was interpreted as an omen foretelling Troy's destruction, and as soon as he was born Paris was exposed on the slopes of Ida to die. As in other myths (Oedipus, Romulus) Paris escaped death and grew up to be a herdsman (1246, 77n). Zeus chose this royal shepherd to judge the beauty contest of the goddesses (see *Background to the story*, p. v).

1255 A beauty competition – and my death The whole story is encapsulated in one line and, to add maximum impact, Iphigeneia's death has been reserved for the end of the line (see **'Helen's guilt'**, p. 54).

They'll kill my daughters in Argos and you two 1225
And me, if I don't obey the goddess' decree.
It is not Menelaus who has enslaved me, child,
I haven't given in to his wish;
But it is Greece, for whom – like it or not –
I must sacrifice you. We are powerless against this. 1230
Greece must be free, as far as lies in you, my child,
And me. We are Greeks. We cannot let
Barbarians strip us of our wives by force.

CLYTAEMNESTRA My child – and you, strangers – I am overwhelmed,
That you must die. Your father commits you to Hades 1235
And runs away.

IPHIGENEIA Oh, mother, oh, we both must sing
The same lament for my fate.
I no longer live or see the light of the sun.

Io, Io! Snow-clad Phrygian glens, hills of Ida, 1240
Where Priam cast his tender baby Paris,
Taken from his mother,
Called a child of Ida by those in Troy,
But destined to die,
Never should you have offered him a home 1245
As a herdsman with his cows
Near the white water, where the springs
Of the Nymphs are found and the meadow
Is alive with fresh flowers and roses and hyacinth
For the goddesses to pick. 1250
There Pallas came and scheming Cypris
And Hera – Cypris glorying in desire and Pallas
In her spear and Hera in the royal bed
Of Lord Zeus – came to a hateful contest,
A beauty competition – and my death. 1255

1265 Zeus should not have breathed The only time that the king of the gods is said to influence the action of the play. For the attribution of events to gods, see 70n, 398n.

1270 Full of suffering, full of suffering Iphigeneia sings of the suffering endured by ephemeral mankind (1271). As her death is approaching, this is reminiscent of heroes in the *Iliad* who often have a moment of philosophical enlightenment before they die (e.g. Patroclus in *Iliad* 16, Hector in *Iliad* 21 and Achilles himself in *Iliad* 24).

- How apt is it that Iphigeneia blames Helen for her death (see also Chorus, 1210)? How far do you think Helen is to blame?
- What are the qualities of this song? What does it add at this point in the story?

FIFTH EPISODE (1277–1487)
Achilles appears with a crowd of soldiers, some carrying his armour (1315). The army, whose menace has so often been mentioned (489, 506–10, 960–1, 1225–6), has now intervened decisively in the action.

Agitated dialogue (1287–1333)
The exchanges between Achilles and Clytaemnestra are in a trochaic metre, rather than the usual iambics, and in the initial dialogue (1288–1333) the *stichomythia* gains pace as the characters speak in half-lines (*analabē*).

The women see soldiers approaching (from Cacoyannis' film Ifigeneia, *1977).*

Artemis has taken me as a sacrifice
To win glory for Greek girls and a crossing to Troy.
O mother, mother, my father has betrayed me
And gone, leaving me abandoned.
In my misery I see that hateful, hateful Helen.   1260
I am murdered, killed in godless slaughter
By my godless father.

Never should Aulis have given anchorage here
To these bronze-beaked ships, this wooden convoy,
Bound for Troy. And Zeus should not have breathed   1265
This hostile expedition, spinning a wind
For the sails to rejoice, bringing grief to some,
To some necessity, a setting out for some,
While others stay behind.
Full of suffering, full of suffering   1270
Is the race of men, born for a day;
And necessity is, they find,
Their unlucky lot.
O Helen, daughter of Tyndareus,
What sorrow, what sorrow   1275
You have brought the Greeks.

CHORUS I pity you. You should never have met such calamity.
IPHIGENEIA Mother, I see a crowd of men approaching.
CLYTAEMNESTRA And Achilles, Thetis' son, the man you came here for.
IPHIGENEIA Open the door, servants, so I can hide.   1280
CLYTAEMNESTRA Why run away, my child?
IPHIGENEIA I am embarrassed to see Achilles.
CLYTAEMNESTRA Why?
IPHIGENEIA The undone marriage makes me ashamed.
CLYTAEMNESTRA No room for modesty in the present situation.   1285
Stay here. Forget your pride, if we can get some help.
ACHILLES Daughter of Leda, poor woman, . . .
CLYTAEMNESTRA How right you are.
ACHILLES There is uproar among the Greeks.

Anarchy and mutiny

Achilles, for all his boastful promises, has been shown to be a 'nothing' (931): he has been attacked by the troops (1297), including his own contingent of Myrmidons (1303). The army is presented as out of control (1303, 1305, 1311). A meeting has taken place, at which Odysseus has been chosen by the soldiers as leader of a contingent to seize Iphigeneia. See Agamemnon's prediction that he would lead a revolt (503–8).

Achilles the hero

Achilles' grandiloquent, impassioned oaths to defend Iphigeneia (909–36) appeared to have been watered down when he advised Clytaemnestra to try to persuade Agamemnon to change his mind (971). But now that persuasion has failed, despite the scornful hostility of the troops (1295–1303) he has come to honour his pledge, to fight for Iphigeneia, alone if necessary (1314–15, 1319).

1322 Sisyphus' son In Homer Odysseus is the son of Laertes (as the Chorus say, 196n). But there was a tradition, which Clytaemnestra knows, that his real father was Sisyphus: that Antikleia, Odysseus' mother, was already pregnant by him when she married Laertes. Odysseus was called 'Sisyphus' son' as an insult in Sophocles' plays *Ajax* and *Philoctetes*. Sisyphus, the king of Corinth, was known as a master of craft and deception (hence perhaps the connection with Odysseus); he also appears in the underworld (*Odyssey* 9) as a sinner, punished by having to push uphill a stone that constantly falls back down. His most famous exploit was to cheat Death, whom he tricked into revealing how his manacles were opened; Sisyphus then locked up Death for a time.

CLYTAEMNESTRA What do you mean? Tell me.   1290

ACHILLES They say that your daughter . . .

CLYTAEMNESTRA This sounds ominous.

ACHILLES That she must be slaughtered.

CLYTAEMNESTRA And no one speaks against it?

ACHILLES I ran into trouble myself.   1295

CLYTAEMNESTRA With whom?

ACHILLES I was pelted with stones.

CLYTAEMNESTRA You were trying to save my child?

ACHILLES Yes.

CLYTAEMNESTRA Who would dare to lay hands on you?   1300

ACHILLES All the Greeks.

CLYTAEMNESTRA Weren't your Myrmidon soldiers there?

ACHILLES They were the first to attack me.

CLYTAEMNESTRA Then we are finished, child.

ACHILLES They jeered – called me the bride's lackey.   1305

CLYTAEMNESTRA What did you say to that?

ACHILLES I said, 'Don't kill my wife to be.'

CLYTAEMNESTRA Quite right.

ACHILLES 'Her father promised her to me.'

CLYTAEMNESTRA And sent for her from Argos.   1310

ACHILLES But I was shouted down.

CLYTAEMNESTRA Crowds are terrifying.

ACHILLES But I will defend you.

CLYTAEMNESTRA You're going to fight, one against many?

ACHILLES These men are carrying my armour.   1315

CLYTAEMNESTRA Bless you for your support.

ACHILLES Yes, we shall have blessings.

CLYTAEMNESTRA So my daughter will not be killed?

ACHILLES Not if it depends on me.

CLYTAEMNESTRA Will someone come to seize her?   1320

ACHILLES A great crowd, led by Odysseus.

CLYTAEMNESTRA Sisyphus' son?

ACHILLES The very one.

1331 Hold on to your daughter It is not clear how this is consistent with Achilles' promise to protect Iphigeneia.

Iphigeneia's transformation

Iphigeneia, who has listened in silence to Achilles and Clytaemnestra, suddenly acquires a new and decisive resolution. No longer is she the pathetic child, pleading for her life (1207–9). She has decided to sacrifice herself, a martyr for Greece; a woman (1358) and a mortal (1360–1) must not thwart the needs of Greece. She is concerned that Achilles should not die (1337–9); she repeats the arguments which Agamemnon used (1212–33) when he declared the sacrifice unavoidable – the demands of the prophecy, the hostility of the army and the call to Panhellenic duty. As with Polyxena in Euripides' *Hecuba*, the rhetoric of her language seems to move into a heroic register (1365n).

Aristotle, writing 80 years after the first performance of the play, drew attention to the change in Iphigeneia, apparently questioning its credibility. Iphigeneia has performed a total *volte-face*.

- How do you understand the change that has taken place? Do the reasons which she gives for changing her mind seem credible?
- Given all the other changes of mind in the play, do you find Aristotle's criticism valid?

The army (from Cacoyannis' film Ifigeneia, *1977).*

CLYTAEMNESTRA Acting on his own, or detailed by the army?

ACHILLES Chosen, and willing. 1325

CLYTAEMNESTRA What a filthy business, to choose a murderer.

ACHILLES But I will stop him.

CLYTAEMNESTRA He'll seize her and take her off, against her will?

ACHILLES Seize her by her golden hair.

CLYTAEMNESTRA What must I do then? 1330

ACHILLES Hold on to your daughter.

CLYTAEMNESTRA I'll do that, to stop her being killed.

ACHILLES It may come to that.

IPHIGENEIA Mother, listen to me. I see your anger with
    Your husband. But it will get you nowhere. It's too hard for us 1335
    To persevere in what's impossible. We must thank
    Our friend for his support. But you must make sure
    He does not fall foul of the army, that he is not ruined
    With no benefit to us. I have been thinking, mother. Hear
    What I have decided. I have resolved to die. 1340
    I want to do it with dignity, in no way
    Ignobly. Look at things as I do, mother. I am right.
    All Greece now looks to me. On me depends
    The passage of the fleet and Troy's destruction.
    Through me the barbarians will pay for Paris' rape of Helen 1345
    By her death. And in future, whatever they may try,
    They'll not be able to abduct the wives of blessed Greece.
    All that I shall achieve by dying. And my fame
    As the liberator of Greece will be revered.
    I must not be a coward. You bore me, a child 1350
    For all the Greeks to share, not for yourself alone.
    Shall ten thousand men, armed with shields,
    And thousands more of oarsmen show their bravery
    When their country is wronged, prepared to face the enemy
    And die for Greece – and will my single life prevent all that? 1355
    How could we argue that is right? And let me make
    A further point. Achilles must not be made to fight
    The whole Greek army and to give his life for a woman.
    One man deserves to live more than ten thousand women.

1365 Greeks should rule barbarians Iphigeneia takes Agamemnon's patriotic rhetoric to a new level (see **'Panhellenic mission'**, p. 82). She sees herself as the liberator (1349) and saviour (1385, 1438) of Greece.

1368 the role of Artemis The Chorus remain unhappy about the sacrifice (see **'Moral decline'**, p. 74).

1369 the gods would have blessed me Achilles is overcome with admiration, but confused. Iphigeneia has shown such noble and pious qualities (1372–4) that now he truly wants her as his wife. Though he believes she is right to submit to the gods' will (1373–4), he tries to subvert her wish for a heroic death.

1390–1 I shall . . . lay / My weapons there Achilles does not don his armour.

- Do you think this is a sign of weakness or of respect for Iphigeneia's wishes?

If Artemis has expressed the wish to have my body,   1360
Shall I stand in her way, a mortal thwart a goddess?
It cannot be. I dedicate my body to Greece.
Sacrifice me and plunder Troy. That will be my memorial
For future years, my children, my marriage and my reputation.
Greeks should rule barbarians, mother, not barbarians   1365
Rule Greeks. They are a race of slaves; we Greeks are free.

CHORUS Young woman, you have a noble nature,
But your fortune and the role of Artemis are all awry.

ACHILLES Child of Agamemnon, the gods would have blessed me,
If I could have married you. I envy Greece   1370
That she has you, and you that you have Greece.
Your words were noble and worthy of your fatherland.
You chose not to fight the gods, who are stronger than you,
And addressed what is right and necessary.
As I contemplate your character, my longing   1375
To have you as my wife grows stronger. You are noble.
I want to help you and take you to my home.
It will be a grief to me – let Thetis hear me –
If I fail to save you. I'll fight the Greeks for you.
Think: it is a dreadful thing to die.   1380

IPHIGENEIA I speak now with fear of no man.
It is enough that Helen pitched men into battle
And into killing, for her beauty. My friend,
Don't die for me, don't kill for me.
Let me, if I can, be the saviour of Greece.   1385

ACHILLES Noble spirit! I cannot say more, if that
Is your decision. Your thoughts are worthy of your birth.
How can I not acknowledge what is true?
But still perhaps you may change your mind.
Listen to what I say. I shall go to the altar and lay   1390
My weapons there; I won't allow, I will prevent
Your dying. Perhaps my words will be of use
To you, when you see the sword at your throat.
I will not let you die misguidedly.

1418 he has a hard struggle ahead See 'Clytaemnestra 2', p. 78.

1420 That was ignoble, unworthy of Atreus Can the irony be unintentional on Clytaemnestra's lips? (See **'Ancestry'**, p. 68.)

Mourning

It was the women's role in the family to wash and dress a corpse for burial; wearing black and with their hair shorn (1401), they would also sing laments and make appropriate libations.

Iphigeneia's nobility 1

Iphigeneia's nobility is praised by the Chorus and Achilles (1367, 1372). Like a true noble's, her thoughts and words are worthy of her ancestry (see **'Ancestry'**, p. 68). She now not only forbids mourning for her death or any sign of grief; she even begs her mother not to hate Agamemnon (1417). Choosing to go alone to her death, she orders the Chorus to sing a hymn to Artemis and herself gives directions for her triumphant martyrdom as saviour of Greece.

I shall go to the goddess' sanctuary with my armour   1395
    And there await your coming.

IPHIGENEIA Mother, why do you weep and say nothing?

CLYTAEMNESTRA I have reason to grieve.

IPHIGENEIA Stop! Don't make me weaken. I have something to ask of you.

CLYTAEMNESTRA Go on! You will suffer no harm from me, child.   1400

IPHIGENEIA Don't cut your hair or wear black clothes.

CLYTAEMNESTRA Why do you say that, when I have lost you, child?

IPHIGENEIA No, you haven't. I am saved, and you will have glory
    because of me.

CLYTAEMNESTRA How? Must I not grieve for your life?

IPHIGENEIA No, there will be no mound raised for me.   1405

CLYTAEMNESTRA But it is the dying, not the tomb, that is remembered.

IPHIGENEIA The altar of the goddess, Zeus' daughter, will be my memorial.

CLYTAEMNESTRA I will do what you ask. You are right.

IPHIGENEIA And fortunate, to be able to serve my country.

CLYTAEMNESTRA What shall I tell your sisters?   1410

IPHIGENEIA Don't dress them in black either.

CLYTAEMNESTRA Am I to give the girls your love?

IPHIGENEIA Say farewell. Bring up Orestes here to be a man, for me.

CLYTAEMNESTRA Take him. Look at him for the last time.

IPHIGENEIA My dearest, you did your best to help your dear ones.   1415

CLYTAEMNESTRA Is there anything I can do for you in Argos?

IPHIGENEIA Don't hate my father. He is your husband.

CLYTAEMNESTRA Because of you he has a hard struggle ahead of him.

IPHIGENEIA It was for Greece, against his will, that he destroyed me.

CLYTAEMNESTRA But by deception. That was ignoble, unworthy of
    Atreus.   1420

IPHIGENEIA Who will escort me, till they seize me by the hair?

CLYTAEMNESTRA I will.

IPHIGENEIA No, that's not right.

CLYTAEMNESTRA I'll hold your robe.

IPHIGENEIA Mother, please! Stay here! That's better for us both.   1425
    Let one of my father's servants take me
    To the field of Artemis, where I'll be sacrificed.

CLYTAEMNESTRA My child, are you going?

IPHIGENEIA Never to return.

Iphigeneia's second song

Iphigeneia seems intoxicated by the occasion. In exalted, euphoric language she celebrates her own self-sacrifice, anticipating posthumous glory as 'the destroyer of Ilium' (1439). A young and innocent girl sacrificed to facilitate a war, she sees herself as a heroine. The traditional epic glorification of warriors and of war has been expressed by the Chorus (see the *Parodos* and 727–51), but the play conveys also war's grim realities, the menace of armies and crowds, its irrationality and the fearful suffering which it entails.

● How do you react to Iphigeneia's exalted patriotism?

1448 O queen, our mother Artemis was a very ancient deity. Her role as protector of all young creatures means that she was originally their mother, an earth goddess (see 92n).

1451 ladies who live across the water The Chorus, who came from across the Euripus.

1457 Mycenae Perseus' mother Danaë was the daughter of Acrisius, the king of Argos (244n). In his colourful life Perseus cut off the head of the Gorgon Medusa and rescued Andromeda from a sea-monster.

1460 a light for Greece This term was used of Achilles too, in the oracle prophesying his future greatness (1026).

1461 I have no regret in dying Iphigeneia had dreaded the thought of dying (1178–9, 1208–9).

1464 another destiny awaits me The ancient Greeks had no universal notion of an afterlife; *Odyssey* 11 is the clearest picture of life after death: the dead all living a shadowy existence in Hades' realm. Iphigeneia is here concerned with her reputation, her wish for her memory to live on and be glorified after death (1462).

Self-sacrifice

Human sacrifice was condemned as uncivilised and abhorrent (1261). In Aeschylus' *Agamemnon* the sacrifice of Iphigeneia is described as a brutal, heartless killing. But *self*-sacrifice could be seen as noble and heroic. In Euripides' *Hecuba*, in which Priam's daughter Polyxena is sacrificed to appease the spirit of the dead Achilles, Polyxena goes willingly to her death, preferring death to the disgrace of slavery and so winning admiration and glory. Iphigeneia in this play and Polyxena transcend the horror of the sacrifice – Artemis can be asked to enjoy it (1481) – and put into perspective the moral failings of those who kill them.

CLYTAEMNESTRA Leaving your mother.   1430

IPHIGENEIA As you know, it's not what you deserve.

CLYTAEMNESTRA Stop! Don't abandon me.

IPHIGENEIA I won't let you cry. Women, sing a hymn
  In praise of Artemis, to mark my fate.
  Let the Greeks be silent, in respect. Someone begin   1435
  The offering, let the fire be lit with purifying offerings.
  And let my father circle the altar. I go to bring
  Salvation to the Greeks and victory.

  Take me, the destroyer of Ilium
     And of the Phrygians.   1440
     Bring crowns of garlands –
  Here is my hair for you to crown –
     And bowls of holy water.
     Dance round the shrine,
  Around the altar for Artemis, our lady.   1445
     For with the blood of my sacrifice
     I shall satisfy the oracle.
     O queen, O queen, our mother,
        I shall weep no tears.
  That is not right at a sacrament.   1450
  Io, Io, ladies who live across the water,
     Join in the hymn to Artemis
  Here where the fleet of ships waits
  In the narrow anchorage of Aulis,
  Eager for the war that depends on me.   1455
     Io, Mother Earth, primeval,
     And Mycenae my homeland . . .

CHORUS You name the place where Perseus lived,
     The work of the Cyclopes' hands?

IPHIGENEIA It nurtured me to be a light for Greece.   1460
     I have no regret in dying.

CHORUS Your glory will never leave you.

IPHIGENEIA Torch of the day, o light of Zeus,
  Another life, another destiny awaits me.
     Farewell, dear light of day.   1465

Hymn to Artemis

Artemis, according to Calchas, has demanded a sacrifice; but this is the first time in the play that her divinity seems to be emphasised. The Chorus – who deplored the sacrifice, seeing it as characteristic of a degenerate society (1038ff, 1368) – now applaud it, even glorifying Agamemnon (1484–7) and praying to Artemis for victory at Troy. They echo Iphigeneia's language and seem swept up in the emotion of the occasion.

1482 the seat of treachery Laomedon, king of Troy, persuaded the gods Poseidon and Apollo to build walls around his city, but when they had finished he cheated them of their promised reward. This explains Poseidon's implacable hatred of Troy in the *Iliad*.

EXODOS (1488–1586)

The final scene is thought by some people, on stylistic grounds, not to have been written by Euripides. There is certainly a resemblance in some details to the account of Polyxena's sacrifice in *Hecuba*. But intrinsically there seems nothing in the ending that so innovative a writer as Euripides could not have written.

1489 Come out and hear what I have to say Messenger 2 enters and summons Clytaemnestra, who must have left the stage during the hymn.

Wall painting from the House of the Tragic Poet, Pompeii (2nd century BC). Iphigeneia is carried by Achilles and Odysseus, Calchas stands on the right, Agamemnon covers his head, left.

CHORUS	Io, Io. See the destroyer of Ilium
	And of the Phrygians
	As she makes her way, her head
	Crowned with garlands,
	See the bowls of holy water.	1470

Watch as she stains the altar of the mighty goddess
With drops of her spilt blood,
Her graceful neck slit in sacrifice.
Your father waits for you,
The sacred bowls with streams of bounteous water, 1475
And the army of the Greeks,
Eager to sail to Troy.
Let us celebrate Artemis,
The daughter of Zeus, queen of the gods,
Asking for a propitious outcome. 1480
Lady, lady, take pleasure in this human sacrifice.
Send against the Trojan land, the seat of treachery,
The army of the Greeks.
And grant that Agamemnon,
Most famous among the spears of Greece, 1485
May wear upon his head
A crown of everlasting glory.

MESSENGER 2 Daughter of Tyndareus, Clytaemnestra,
Come out and hear what I have to say.
CLYTAEMNESTRA I heard your voice. I'm here, afraid 1490
And wretched, distraught with dread.
You've not come bringing another catastrophe,
On top of what we suffer?
MESSENGER 2 I have something wonderful, extraordinary,
To tell you, about your daughter. 1495
CLYTAEMNESTRA Then don't hesitate. Quick, tell me!
MESSENGER 2 Dear mistress, you will hear everything in detail.
I'll start at the beginning, unless my recollection
Falters as I speak and trips my tongue.

1503 The crowd of Argives surged forward The behaviour of the Greek army here is reminiscent of Clytaemnestra's first arrival (409–12). Whether curious or menacing, we are not to forget their presence.

1505 He let out a wail The Messenger's description of the grief-stricken father is reflected in a wall painting from Pompeii, p. 98.

Iphigeneia's nobility 2

Iphigeneia enters and freely offers herself to the soldiers for the sacrifice (1509–10). Selfless and sublime, her reported speech (1508–15) has the same heroic tone as in the fifth episode (1340–66). In saying that she does not need to be held down for the sacrifice (1514), she not only preserves her dignity (1341) but observes the needs of the ritual: a sacrifice was considered successful only if the victim was seen to die willingly or at least without a struggle. This is a version very different from the account in Aeschylus' *Agamemnon*, where Iphigeneia has to be hauled over the altar like an animal for the sacrifice.

- Is there an element of conscious role-playing in Iphigeneia's attitude? Do we admire her or feel pity?
- Does Agamemnon's grief seem genuine to you?

1516 Everyone was transfixed The nobility and bravery displayed by Iphigeneia has an almost magical effect on the army; they appear to be tamed and disciplined. Iphigeneia seems to transcend her mortal status.

1518 Talthybius The herald of the army (see 95n). Here he calls for reverent silence as noise was considered a bad omen (1435).

Calchas' role in the sacrifice

Calchas not only plays the soothsayer at the sacrifice; he is also the priest who will perform the rites, preparing the blade and crowning the girl with the sacrificial garlands (1520–3). See **'Calchas' prophecy'**, p. 10; 1221.

Achilles' *volte-face*

Achilles has, without explanation, abandoned his emphatic promise to save Iphigeneia (see 1379, 1391–2). His oath is apparently forgotten and he is prominent as an assistant in the sacrificial ceremony. He has fallen into line. No doubt his explanation would be his admiration of Iphigeneia (1372–4, 1386) and his wish to serve the Greek cause (928–9). He would also thus placate the rabid troops and preserve his own position.

1526 Daughter of Zeus, who kill wild animals Achilles plays down the sacrifice, hiding it amongst Artemis' other areas of responsibility, here as goddess of hunting and of the moon.

When we came to the grove of Artemis, Zeus' daughter,   1500
And the gardens full of flowers, where the Greek army
Was assembled, as we led in your daughter, suddenly
The crowd of Argives surged forward. And when Lord Agamemnon
Saw the girl making her way into the grove to the sacrifice,
He let out a wail and, throwing back his head,   1505
He burst into tears, hiding his eyes with his robe.
She stood beside him, her father, and said
'Father, here I am. I offer here my body
Of my free will to them, to take to the altar
Of the goddess and to sacrifice for my country   1510
And for the whole of Greece, if that is the goddess' word.
I wish you success. May you triumph in war
And come back safely to your homeland.
Because I do this for you, let no Greek touch me!
I will say nothing. I will offer my throat without flinching.'   1515
That was all. Everyone was transfixed as they heard
The brave words of the girl and her nobility.
Standing in the middle, Talthybius, whose role it was,
Called for respect and silence from the troops.
Calchas the seer took from its sheath his sword,   1520
Its blade sharp to the touch, and placed it
In a basket of beaten gold. And then
He crowned her head with garlands.
The son of Peleus took the basket and the holy water
And ran round the altar; then he said,   1525
'Daughter of Zeus, who kill wild animals
And spin the light of the moon by night,
Receive this sacrifice which we give to you –
We, the army of the Greeks and Agamemnon –
The pure blood from the throat of this beautiful maiden,   1530
And grant that the fleet may sail unharmed
And that the citadel of Troy fall to our spears.'
The sons of Atreus stood, and the whole army,
Their eyes cast down.

1538 suddenly there was a miracle The play, full of unexpected twists, has one more surprise. While the spectators' heads are bowed (1534, 1537), the miraculous exchange takes place.

1544 A deer lay gasping on the ground It is fitting that Iphigeneia has been replaced at the crucial moment of death by a deer, Artemis' sacred animal. It is almost as if a metamorphosis has occurred.

1547 Calchas The supreme master of ceremonies, Calchas presides over the sacrifice and also decides how the miraculous transformation is to be interpreted (1548ff).

Supernatural intervention

Euripides quite often ended a play by using a deity to resolve the plot (*Hippolytus, Electra, Orestes, Bacchae*); in *Medea* Medea is swept away in the chariot of Helios, the sun god (153n). Euripides had also written two plays in which traditional myths had been miraculously changed: in *Helen* Helen does not go to Troy at all (see 763n); and in *Iphigeneia among the Taurians* Euripides had employed the idea of Artemis rescuing Iphigeneia from the sacrifice and making her a priestess in her cult in a savage land. In our play the supernatural intervention is not shown, but related – by a Messenger sent by Agamemnon.

1566 Let go your grief and anger at your husband Clytaemnestra's anger has been obvious to everyone (1334, 1417). The Messenger has been sent by Agamemnon (1561) to reassure her. All that is required to complete the happy ending is that she should rejoice at the honour shown to her daughter (1569) and forget her resentment of Agamemnon.

Happy ending?

The Messenger's speech has a celebratory tone, designed to cheer and comfort Clytaemnestra. The characters of the play have struggled to control events. No one, apart from the army – and Iphigeneia after her *volte-face* – really wanted the sacrifice to happen, but Agamemnon has made his choice and the traditional narrative of the myth can go on unaffected. Artemis is seen now as a benevolent deity, who didn't really want a human sacrifice (1551–2), but rewards the Greeks for Iphigeneia's noble offer. The power of the goddess is asserted, heroism and patriotism are glorified. There is a cost, in the sacrifice of a human life, but even that is mollified by Iphigeneia's ascension to the gods. The ways of the gods may be mysterious (1567), but they are real, and reassuring. Certainly the Chorus are happy (1570).

The priest took his sword and said a prayer. He looked   1535
To see where he would strike the throat.
I was overwhelmed by grief and bowed my head.
But suddenly there was a miracle.
We all could clearly hear the sound of the blow,
But nobody could tell where the girl had gone.   1540
The priest cried out, the whole army echoed him,
As they saw, to their astonishment, a sign sent by a god,
Something we could not believe, although we saw it:
A deer lay gasping on the ground, enormous
And extraordinary to see, and its blood   1545
Ran all over the altar of the goddess.
And Calchas, rejoicing as you can imagine, cried:
'Leaders of this united army of the Greeks,
Do you see this sacrifice, which the goddess
Has offered at the altar, a deer that runs the hills?   1550
This she is happy with, rather than the girl,
So that she does not pollute the altar with noble blood.
This sacrifice she has received with delight and grants us
A fair wind for our crossing and our attack on Troy.
Let each sailor take heart at this and go to his ship.   1555
This very day we must leave the sheltered bay
Of Aulis and brave the Aegean swell.'
When all the sacrifice was reduced to ash in Hephaestus' flame,
He prayed for a favourable outcome,
That the army should have a safe return.   1560
Agamemnon sends me to report all this and to say
What honour the gods have conferred,
Undying glory throughout Greece.
I was there and tell you what I saw. It's clear
Your daughter has been transported to the gods.   1565
Let go your grief and anger at your husband.
The ways of the gods surprise us mortals:
They save those whom they love. This day
Has seen your daughter die and live again.

The Messenger's speech

The Messenger speech is a traditional feature found in most Greek tragedies, in which an eye-witness recounts events that have happened away from the play's setting. This news is usually horrific or exciting, displaying various narrative techniques to make the speech dramatic. These techniques, including direct speech and specific details, allow the actor freedom to 'perform' the speech with heightened drama and tension.

Clytaemnestra's reaction

Had Artemis herself appeared (as she does at the end of *Hippolytus*), Clytaemnestra would not have been able to question the 'miracle'. But wary, no doubt, after so many false messages, her response, in a series of questions addressed to the absent Iphigeneia (1572–5), is sceptical. She questions the truth of the story.

- What aspects of the Messenger's speech might make Clytaemnestra suspicious?

1576 Lord Agamemnon Agamemnon enters to say the briefest of farewells. He does not attempt to comfort Clytaemnestra in her grief or have a conversation with her.

1580 Take this little fellow and go home Iphigeneia used her baby brother Orestes to gain sympathy (see 1200). Here the child seems to be the embodiment of family life, as Agamemnon bids his wife to go home and carry on as normal. There is a sinister irony as Orestes will grow up to be an atypical son towards his mother, murdering her in revenge for her murder of Agamemnon upon his return from Troy.

The ending of the play

Although they do not have – as often – a song to sing as they leave the stage, the final words of the play belong to the Chorus. Their cheerful words, as they send Agamemnon on his way, have a grim irony. On his return from Troy he will bring the Trojan priestess Cassandra with him as plunder (1586), and he will be murdered by Clytaemnestra. See also **'Assessment of the play'** and **'A radical reading of the play'** (p. 106).

- Do you admire or feel sympathy for anyone at the end of the play?
- What effect would you aim at in staging the ending? Might the focus be on Clytaemnestra and her rejection of the Messenger's account? How would Clytaemnestra, Agamemnon and the Chorus leave at the end? Who would leave last?

CHORUS I rejoice to hear this news. He says   1570
    Your child is alive and living with the gods.
CLYTAEMNESTRA My child, have the gods stolen you away?
            How am I to address you? How can I not say
                That these are false tales to reassure me,
                    To spare me my grievous mourning for you?   1575

CHORUS Here comes Lord Agamemnon
    To tell you the same tale.
AGAMEMNON My wife, we can feel blessed in our daughter!
    Truly she has been welcomed into heaven.
    Take this little fellow and go home. The army   1580
    Is looking to embark. Farewell. It will be
    Some time before you hear from me in Troy.
    I hope things go well for you.
CHORUS I wish you well, son of Atreus, for your voyage
            To the land of Phrygia and for your return,   1585
                Bringing from Troy the finest plunder.

Iphigeneia dressed for her sacrifice (from Cacoyannis' film
Ifigeneia, *1977).*

Assessment of the play

The play, about the prologue to a war, was written at the end of a long and destructive war. It explores an ethical dilemma, famous in mythology. Euripides characteristically strips the story of its heroic or exemplary qualities, showing weak, fallible men in a fumbling attempt to control events. Agamemnon, rejecting the claims of love and familial duties, abandons his moral judgement through fear of the army and Odysseus and surrenders to 'necessity'. The play contains exciting twists of plot, scenes of deep emotion, pathos and psychological depth. The characters, under the stress of extreme pressure, vacillate in the conflict between their personal and public duties and ambitions. Played against the background of an anarchic, menacing army and war fever, it is pulsating drama.

- Is the 'point' of the play that, however ineffective or corrupt men are, there are still heroes – or rather heroines – and patriotism can still be celebrated and there are powerful deities in heaven? How can the 'comforting' denouement of the sacrifice be reconciled with the unedifying presentation of the Greek leaders?
- Or is the strength and main focus of the play its examination of human nature under extremes of stress? If so, does this make the ending contrived and cynical? Does that matter?
- It has been argued (by Don Taylor, see below) that Iphigeneia deserves pity as an impressionable girl who has been manipulated and exploited by war-mongers. Do you agree?
- What aspects of the play do you think give it relevance and appeal to an audience today?

A radical reading of the play

Don Taylor – in the preface to his translation of the play (used for the National Theatre production, London, 2004) – suggests that the degraded atmosphere of the Greek camp, whose characters reflect the self-interest and violence of Euripides' own contemporaries, corrupts the two virtuous women. Clytaemnestra is turned from an exemplary wife into an avenging fury and Iphigeneia into a deluded 'heroine', the dupe of patriotic rhetoric, sacrificing herself willingly for the ambition of the generals. It is a world where no one, not even the priest (495), is trustworthy; all are capable of deceit. So when the Messenger relates the events of the sacrifice, does he tell the truth? What exactly happened? Only Calchas perhaps was watching (1535). Is Calchas' explanation the 'public relations' version, the official story, to cover the gruesome killing, to save Agamemnon's face, the crowning deceit of the play – which does not fool Clytaemnestra (1574–5)?

Synopsis of the play

PROLOGUE (1–157)

Agamemnon is alone, agitated and pacing the stage. The Old Man comes out of the tent and asks him what the problem is. Agamemnon explains that the priest Calchas has prophesied that the Greek army will not be able to sail and capture Troy unless he sacrifices his daughter Iphigeneia to Artemis. Agamemnon has already sent a letter to his wife Clytaemnestra, asking her to send their daughter for a supposed ceremony of betrothal to Achilles (Achilles has no idea about this). Now he is having second thoughts about the sacrifice, and he has written a second letter to cancel the instructions of the first. He entrusts this to the Old Man.

PARODOS (158–279)

The Chorus (young, married Greek women from Chalcis, close to Aulis) enter. They have come to see for themselves the Greek heroes of whom their husbands have spoken.

FIRST EPISODE (280–517)

The Old Man and Menelaus enter the stage arguing. Menelaus has intercepted the Old Man and has opened the second letter before it was delivered. Agamemnon, disturbed by the commotion, comes out of the tent. Menelaus accuses Agamemnon of going back on his word to sacrifice his daughter. The brothers are arguing when a Messenger arrives to announce the arrival of Clytaemnestra and their children. Menelaus backs down and agrees that Agamemnon must not kill his child. However, Agamemnon has changed his mind now, and says that he must, as he is scared of the army. Agamemnon asks Menelaus to ensure that Clytaemnestra does not hear about the planned sacrifice.

FIRST CHORAL ODE (518–81)

The Chorus sing of sexual desire, modesty and self-restraint. They then tell the story of Paris and Helen and their unbridled passion, which has brought their homelands to the brink of war. They finish their song by welcoming Clytaemnestra and her entourage.

SECOND EPISODE (582–726)

Clytaemnestra, Iphigeneia and the baby Orestes descend from their carriage. Iphigeneia is keen to see her father, who enters the stage upon their arrival. Father and daughter converse briefly about the impending war, and he sends her into the tent. Clytaemnestra asks for more information about the bridegroom, which Agamemnon gives. He tries to send Clytaemnestra back to Argos as an army camp is no place for women, but she refuses to relinquish her role as mother of the bride-to-be. She goes into the tent to make plans for the betrothal ceremony. Agamemnon goes off to see Calchas for further advice about Artemis' wishes.

SECOND CHORAL ODE (727–65)

The Chorus sing of the destruction of Troy which is to come, the savage fighting and the future which awaits the Trojan women.

THIRD EPISODE (766–994)

Achilles approaches the tent, in response to the soldiers' unrest, to ask Agamemnon whether they will sail to Troy or abandon the expedition. Clytaemnestra comes out of the tent to introduce herself to her future son-in-law. Achilles is shocked to hear that he is supposed to marry Iphigeneia; he says that they have both been deceived by Agamemnon. The Old Man appears at the door of the tent but is afraid to come out. When he is finally persuaded, he reveals Agamemnon's intention to sacrifice his daughter. Clytaemnestra begs Achilles to defend Iphigeneia. Achilles swears that Iphigeneia will not be killed; he is angry that Agamemnon used his name without permission. He advises Clytaemnestra to try to persuade Agamemnon to rethink his plans. If he persists, then Achilles will protect her. Both leave the stage.

THIRD CHORAL ODE (995–1055)

The Chorus sing of the joyous wedding feast of Peleus and Thetis and the prophecy about Thetis' son. Then they imagine the sacrifice of Iphigeneia, and finally comment upon man's inability to escape the anger of the gods.

FOURTH EPISODE (1056–1236)

Clytaemnestra comes out of the tent in search of her husband, who enters the stage from the side. He, unaware that his wife knows of his plans to kill Iphigeneia, asks her to summon the girl as she is needed to attend the betrothal sacrifice. Iphigeneia comes out, carrying her baby brother, as her mother instructed. Clytaemnestra asks Agamemnon directly whether he plans to kill her, and Agamemnon, distressed, does not deny it. Clytaemnestra begs him to reconsider, and the Chorus echo her wish. Iphigeneia also begs him to save her, but he explains that the army are desperate to go to war to punish Troy. It is for Greece, he says, that she must be sacrificed. Clytaemnestra is overcome with grief.

MONODY (1237–76)

Iphigeneia sings a song of lamentation, which expresses her isolation. She compares her situation with that of Paris when he was young, before turning to blame Helen.

FIFTH EPISODE (1277–1487)

A group of soldiers approaches, with Achilles. He tells Clytaemnestra that although he tried to defend Iphigeneia, the army were too hostile, and Odysseus and a mob are on their way to take Iphigeneia to the sacrifice. Iphigeneia has listened to their exchange and has changed her mind; she is now resolved to die for Greece's sake. Achilles admires her nobility and expresses his desire to marry her. He says that he will fight the Greeks on her behalf, and he goes off to the altar where the sacrifice is to take place to defend her. Iphigeneia tells her mother not to grieve for her and begs her to stay away from the sacrifice. As she leaves the stage, she sings a song of her own heroic and patriotic self-sacrifice. The Chorus sing a hymn to Artemis.

EXODOS (1488–1586)

A Messenger arrives, sent by Agamemnon, to tell Clytaemnestra about the sacrifice. At the moment of slaughter Iphigeneia vanished and a deer appeared in her place; the girl has been transported to the gods. The Chorus rejoice. Clytaemnestra cannot believe the news. Agamemnon hurries in and instructs his wife to go home. He bids her a hasty farewell as the army is about to set sail. The Chorus send him on his way with their best wishes.

Pronunciation of names

To attempt an authentic pronunciation of classical Greek names would present great difficulties. It is perhaps easiest to accept the conventional anglicised versions of the familiar names (e.g. Ares, Zeus). The key below offers help with all the names of the play, which will produce a reasonable overall consistency. Note that the stress occurs on the italicised syllable.

KEY

ay – as in 'hay' ō – long 'o' as in 'go'
ē – as in 'hair' ī – as in 'die'

Achilles	A-*kill*-ees	Dardanus	*Dar*-da-nus
Aeacus	*Ee*-a-kus	Diomedes	Dī-o-*mee*-deez
Aegean	Ee-*jee*-an	Dioscuri	Di-*os*-cu-ree
Aegina	Ee-*jī*-na	Echinades	E-*khi*-na-deez
Aenianian	Ee-ni-*ay*-ni-an	Elis	*Ee*-lis
Agamemnon	A-ga-*mem*-non	Epeians	E-*pee*-ans
Ajax	*Ay*-jax	Eros	*Ee*-ros
Alpheus	Al-*fay*-us	Euboea	Yu-*bee*-a
Aphrodite	A-fro-*dī*-te	Eumelus	Yu-*mee*-lus
Apidanus	A-*pi*-dan-us	Euripus	Yu-*rī*-pus
Apollo	A-*pol*-lo	Eurotas	Yu-*rō*-tas
Ares	*Ē*-reez	Eurytus	*Yu*-ri-tus
Arethusa	A-re-*thyu*-sa	Ganymede	*Ga*-ni-meed
Argos	*Ar*-gos	Gerana	Ge-*rar*-na
Artemis	*Ar*-tem-is	Gouneus	*Goo*-nyus
Asopus	A-*sō*-pus	Hades	*Hay*-deez
Atreus	*Ay*-tri-us	Helios	*Hee*-li-os
Aulis	*Ow*-lis	Hephaestus	He-*fīs*-tus
Bacchus	*Bak*-kus	Hera	*Hee*-ra
Boeotian	Bee*ō*-shun	Hermione	Her-*mī*-o-ny
Cadmus	*Kad*-mus	Ida	*Ī*-da
Calchas	*Kal*-kas	Ilium	*Ī*-li-um
Capaneus	*Ka*-pa-nyus	Inachus	*Ī*-na-kus
Cassandra	Kas-*san*-dra	Io	*Ī*-ō
Centaur	*Sen*-tor	Iphigeneia	Ī-fi-je-*nī*-a
Chalcis	*Kal*-kis	Laertes	Lay-*er*-teez
Cheiron	*Kī*-rōn	Leda	*Lee*-da
Clytaemnestra	Klī-tem-*nes*-tra	Leitus	*Lay*-tus
Cyclopes	Sī-*klō*-peez	Locrian	*Loc*-ri-an
Cypris	*Ki*-pris	Lydian	*Li*-di-an

Meges *Me*-geez
Mekisteus Mē-*kis*-tyus
Menelaus Me-ne-*lay*-us
Meriones *Mee*-ri-o-neez
Mycenae *Mī*-see-nee
Myrmidons *Mer*-mi-dons
Nereid *Nee*-re-id
Nereus *Nee*-ryus
Nestor *Nes*-tor
Nireus *Nī*-ryus
Odysseus O-*dis*-se-us
Oileus *Oi*-lyus
Oinone Oi-*nō*-nee
Orestes O-*res*-teez
Orpheus *Or*-fe-us
Palamedes Pa-la-*mee*-deez
Pallas *Pal*-las
Paris *Pa*-ris
Peleus *Pee*-le-us
Pelion *Pee*-li-on
Pelops *Pe*-lops
Pergamon *Per*-ga-mon
Perseus *Per*-si-us
Pharsalus *Far*-sa-lus
Pheretias Fe-*re*-ti-as
Phoebe *Fee*-bee

Phrygia *Fri*-ji-a
Phthia *Fthi*-a
Phyleus *Fī*-lyus
Pleiades *Plī*-a-deez
Poseidon Po-*sī*-don
Priam *Prī*-am
Protesilaus Prō-te-si-*lay*-us
Pylos *Pī*-los
Salamis *Sa*-la-mis
Simois *Si*-mō-is
Sipylos *Si*-pi-los
Sisyphus *Sis*-i-fus
Sthenelus *Sthe*-ne-lus
Talaus *Ta*-lay-us
Talthybius Tal-*thi*-bi-us
Tantalus *Tan*-ta-lus
Taphians *Ta*-fi-ans
Telamon Te-la-mon
Theseus *Thee*-se-us
Thessaly *The*-sa-li
Thestius *Thes*-ti-us
Thetis *The*-tis
Thronium *Thro*-ni-um
Tyndareus *Tin*-da-ryus
Zeus Zyoos

Introduction to the Greek Theatre

Theātron, the Greek word that gave us 'theatre' in English, meant both 'viewing place' and the assembled viewers. These ancient viewers (*theātai*) were in some ways very different from their modern counterparts. For a start, they were participants in a religious festival, and they went to watch plays only on certain days in the year, when shows were put on in honour of Dionysus. At Athens, where drama developed many of its most significant traditions, the main Dionysus festival, held in the spring, was one of the most important events in the city's calendar, attracting large numbers of citizens and visitors from elsewhere in the Greek world. It is not known for certain whether women attended; if any did, they were more likely to be visitors than the wives of Athenian citizens.

The festival was also a great sporting occasion. Performances designed to win the god's favour needed spectators to witness and share in the event, just as the athletic contests did at Olympia or Delphi, and one of the ways in which the spectators got involved was through competition. What they saw were three sets of three tragedies plus a satyr play, five separate comedies and as many as twenty song-and-dance performances called dithyrambs, put on in honour of Dionysus by choruses representing the different 'tribes' into which the citizen body was divided. There was a contest for each different event, with the dithyramb choruses divided into men's and boys' competitions, and a panel of judges determined the winners. The judges were appointed to act on behalf of the city; no doubt they took some notice of the way the audience responded on each occasion. Attendance at these events was on a large scale: we should be thinking of football crowds rather than typical theatre audiences in the modern world.

Like football matches, dramatic festivals were open-air occasions, and the performances were put on in daylight rather than with stage lighting in a darkened auditorium. The ideal performance space in these circumstances was a hollow hillside to seat spectators, with a flat area at the bottom (*orchēstra*) in which the chorusmen could spread out for their dancing and singing and which could be closed off by a stage-building (*skēnē*) acting simultaneously as backdrop, changing room and sounding board. Effective acoustics and good sight-lines were achieved by the kind of design represented in Fig. A on page 113, the theatre of Dionysus at Athens. The famous stone theatre at Epidaurus (Fig. B), built about 330 BC, and often taken as typical, has a circular *orchēstra*, but in the fifth century it was normal practice for theatres to have a low wooden stage in front of the *skēnē*, for use by the actors, who also interacted with the chorus in the *orchēstra*.

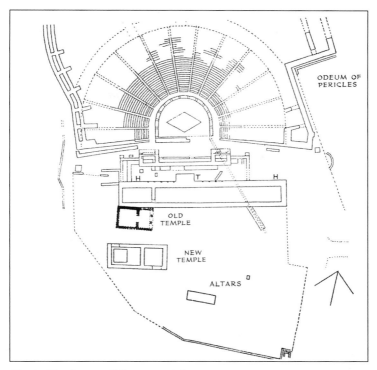

Fig. A. The theatre of Dionysus at Athens.

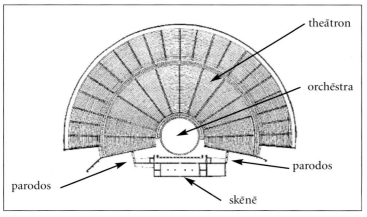

Fig. B. The theatre at Epidaurus (fourth century BC).

Song and dance by choruses and the accompanying music of the piper were integral to all these types of performance and not just to the dithyramb. In tragedy there were 12 (later 15) chorusmen, in comedy 24, and in dithyramb 50; plays were often named after their chorus: Aeschylus' *Persians*, Euripides' *Bacchae*, Aristophanes' *Birds* are familiar examples. The rhythmic movements, groupings and singing of the chorus contributed crucially to the overall impact of each show, ensuring that there was always an animated stage picture even when only one or two actors were in view. The practice of keeping the number of speaking actors normally restricted to three, with doubling of roles by the same actor where necessary, looks odd at first sight, but it makes sense in the special circumstance of Greek theatrical performance. Two factors are particularly relevant: first the use of masks, which was probably felt to be fundamental to shows associated with the cult of Dionysus and which made it easy for an actor to take more than one part within a single play, and second the need to concentrate the audience's attention by keeping the number of possible speakers limited. In a large, open acting area some kind of focusing device is important if the spectators are always to be sure where to direct their gaze. The Greek plays that have survived, particularly the tragedies, are extremely economical in their design, with no sub-plots or complications in the action which audiences might find distracting or confusing. Acting style, too, seems to have relied on large gestures and avoidance of fussy detail; we know from the size of some of the surviving theatres that many spectators would be sitting too far away to catch small-scale gestures or stage business. Some plays make powerful use of props, like Ajax's sword, Philoctetes' bow, or the head of Pentheus in *Bacchae*, but all these are carefully chosen to be easily seen and interpreted.

Above all, actors seem to have depended on their highly trained voices in order to captivate audiences and stir their emotions. By the middle of the fifth century there was a prize for the best actor in the tragic competition, as well as for the playwright and the financial sponsor of the performance (*chorēgos*), and comedy followed suit a little later. What was most admired in the leading actors who were entitled to compete for this prize was the ability to play a series of different and very demanding parts in a single day and to be a brilliant singer as well as a compelling speaker of verse: many of the main parts involve solo songs or complex exchanges between actor and chorus. Overall, the best plays and performances must have offered audiences a great charge of energy and excitement: the chance to see a group of chorusmen dancing and singing in a sequence of different guises, as young maidens, old counsellors, ecstatic maenads, and exuberant satyrs; to watch scenes in which supernatural beings – gods, Furies, ghosts – come into contact with human beings; to listen to intense debates and hear the blood-curdling offstage cries that heralded the arrival of a messenger with an account of terrifying deeds within, and then to see the bodies brought out and witness the lamentations. Far more 'happened' in most plays than we can easily imagine from the bare text on the page; this must help to account for the continuing appeal of drama throughout antiquity and across the Greco-Roman world.

From the fourth century onwards dramatic festivals became popular wherever there were communities of Greek speakers, and other gods besides Dionysus were honoured with performances of plays. Actors, dancers and musicians organised themselves for professional touring – some of them achieved star status and earned huge fees – and famous old plays were revived as part of the repertoire. Some of the plays that had been first performed for Athenian citizens in the fifth century became classics for very different audiences – women as well as men, Latin speakers as well as Greeks – and took on new kinds of meaning in their new environment. But theatre was very far from being an antiquarian institution: new plays, new dramatic forms like mime and pantomime, changes in theatre design, staging, masks and costumes all demonstrate its continuing vitality in the Hellenistic and Roman periods. Nearly all the Greek plays that have survived into modern times are ones that had a long theatrical life in antiquity; this perhaps helps to explain why modern actors, directors and audiences have been able to rediscover their power.

For further reading: entries in *Oxford Classical Dictionary* (3rd edition) under 'theatre staging, Greek' and 'tragedy, Greek'; J.R. Green, 'The theatre', Ch. 7 of *The Cambridge Ancient History, Plates to Volumes V and VI*, Cambridge, 1994; Richard Green and Eric Handley, *Images of the Greek Theatre*, London, 1995; Rush Rehm, *Greek Tragic Theatre*, London and New York, 1992; P.E. Easterling (ed.), *The Cambridge Companion to Greek Tragedy*, Cambridge, 1997; David Wiles, *Tragedy in Athens*, Cambridge, 1997.

Pat Easterling

Time line

Dates of selected authors and extant works

12th Century BC	**The Trojan war**	
8th Century BC	**HOMER**	• *The Iliad* • *The Odyssey*
5th Century BC		
490–479	**The Persian wars**	
431–404	**The Peloponnesian wars**	
c. 525/4–456/5	**AESCHYLUS**	(In probable order.)
472		• *Persians*
		• *Seven against Thebes*
		• *Suppliants*
456		• ***Oresteia Trilogy:***
		Agamemnon, Choephoroi
		Eumenides
		• *Prometheus Bound*
c. 496/5–406	**SOPHOCLES**	(Undated plays are in
		alphabetical order.)
		• *Ajax* • *Oedipus Tyrannus*
		• *Antigone* • *Trachiniae*
		• *Electra*
409		• *Philoctetes*
401 (posthumous)		• *Oedipus at Colonus*
c. 490/80–407/6	**EURIPIDES**	(In probable order.)
438 (1st production 455)		• *Alcestis*
431		• *Medea*
		• *Heradeidae*
428		• *Hippolytus*
		• *Andromache*
		• *Hecuba*
		• *Suppliant Women*
		• *Electra*
415		• *Trojan Women*
		• *Heracles*
		• *Iphigenia among the Taurians*
412		• *Helen*
		• *Ion*
409		• *Phoenissae*
?408		• *Orestes*
		• *Cyclops* (satyr-play)
?406–5		• *Bacchae*
		• *Iphigenia at Aulis*
460/50–*c.* 386	**ARISTOPHANES**	(Selected works.)
411		• *Thesmophoriazusae*
		• *Lysistrata*
405		• *Frogs*
4th Century BC	**ARISTOTLE**	(Selected works.)
384–322		• *The Art of Poetry*

Index

Bold numbers refer to pages. Other numbers are line references.

Iphigeneia: appeal to her father
614–58, **80**, 1170–1209;
attitude to death 1177–9, **82**,
1207–9, 1340, 1461; as a
heroine **96**; innocence 130,
644; nobility 1341–66, **94**,
1403–39, 1462, **100**; sacrifice
72, 1038–55; self-sacrifice
1460, 1508–15; songs **84**, **96**;
supplication 1175–6;
transformation into a deer
102, 1544–69; transformation
of character **90**, 1340–65
Ifigeneia (film) **viii**, **48**, **86**, **90**, **105**

Laertes 196
Laomedon 1482
leadership 17–23, 85–7, **26**, **28**,
356–8
Leda, children of **6**, 49–51
libations **6**, 61
life after death 1464
looms 756
lust for war 773, 1222

marriage customs **32**, 416–21,
691, 995–8: bride's dress 869;
dowries **6**, 47, 586; role of
bride's mother **50**, 701–7;
wedding feasts **12**, 121, **70**
marriage of Peleus and Thetis **48**,
675, 995–1037
Meges 260
Mekisteus' son 230
Menelaus 71, 76–80, 107, 246:
change of mind **34**; entry 280;
family feelings **34**, 460–78;
status 291, 295, 308; potential
for violence 283, 289, 296, 494
Meriones 194
Messengers **30**, 1489n, **104**
moderation (*sōphrosynē*) **40**, 887
monody **84**, **108**
moral decline **68**, **74**
motherhood **62**

mourning **94**
Muses 763, 1001
mutiny **88**
Mycenae 244, 1457
Myrmidons 222, 778

names 991: of parents **58**;
pronunciation **110–1**
necessity 1214, 1230: yoke of 425
nemesis **4**
Nereids 226, 601, 1015
Nereus 1022
Nestor 251
New Comedy **46**, **56**
Nireus 198
nobility **4**, **28**, 479, 788n

oaths **6**, 59, **28**, 382–3, **66**, 966–7
ode (*stasimon*) **40**, **52**, **70**, **107**,
108
Odysseus 107, 196, **38**, 499–508,
88, 1321–9
Oileus, Ajax son of 186, 242
Oinone 673
Old Man **58**, **60**: honesty and
trustworthiness 45; loyalty 835
orchēstra **112**
Orestes 595–9, 1076, 1200, 1413,
1580n
Orpheus 1170

Palamedes 189
Pallas Athene 234–5
Panhellenic mission 353, **28**, **30**,
82, 1365–6
parodos **14**, **22**, **107**, **112**
parents: and children 661–3;
children addressed by names
of **58**; relationships with
children **46**
Paris 550–66, **84**: cursed by
Agamemnon 447; disrespect of
guest-friendship 76; and Helen
75–7, 171, 560–3; herdsman
77, 550–6, 1246; judge of

Paris (*cont.*)
    beauty contest 72; judgement
      of **v**; and Priam 1241
Peleus **v**, **48**, **70**
Pelion, Mount 679, 999
Peloponnesian War **28**, **54**
Pelops **36**, 452, 1191–2
persuasion **68**
Pharsalus 776
philoi (friends) **24**, **30**, **62**, **78**
Phrygia 627
piety (*eusebeia*) **4**
pipes (musical instruments) 553
Plot **58**
Priam 1241
Prologue **2**, **107**
Protesilaus 189
Pylos 250
Pythia 1024

religion, Greek (see also *gods*) **4**:
    respect for the gods 24, **50**, 723
reputation, importance of **28**, **64**
responsibility, burden of **2**, 17–23
rhetoric 311n, **30**, 1126–67, **80**

sacrifices **6**, **32**, **46**: animal **46**; and
    betrothal of Helen 60; human
    10, 91–2, **72**, 1261, **96**, 1481,
    100; of Iphigeneia 647, 1038ff.;
    need for sacrifice at Aulis
    89–94, 1220–1; ritual 919–20,
    1039; and weddings 869n,
    1038, 1069–72
Salamis 188
self-sacrifice **96**
ships **18**, **22**
Simois 727
Sipylos, Mount 916
Sirius (Dog Star) 6
Sisyphus 1322
skēnē **112**
sophistry **60**, 311n

spirit (*alastōr*) 842, 911
spirit (*daimōn*) 426
staff (sceptre) of office 289, 399
stars 6
stasimon (ode) **40**, **52**, **70**, **107**,
    108
Sthenelus 231
stichomythia **22**, 280–311, **46**, **58**,
    820–63, **86**
suitors' oath **28**
supernatural intervention **102**,
    398, 993
supplications **60**, **66**, **80** 1175

tablets, writing 35
Talthybius 95, 1518n
Tantalus **36**, 479, 1108–17, **76**
Taphos 260
Telamon, Ajax son of 186, 264
theatre, Greek **112–5**
Theseus 233
Thetis **v**, **48**, **70**
timē (honour) **28**
Troy (see also *Ilium*) **8**, 1482: fall
    of 727–59
Tyndareus **6**, **46**, 56–8, 990–1,
    1115

weaving 756
wedding customs *see* marriage
    customs
women 1359: in army camp 709;
    behaviour 652; motherhood
    62; mourning responsibilities
    94, 1401; prisoners-of-war
    755; weaving 756
writing tablets 35

xenia **8**

yoke of necessity 425

Zeus **48**, 944–5n, 1265n